The Child With Special Needs

The Child
with
Special Needs

Letters and Essays on
Curative Education

Karl König

Floris Books

Karl König Archive, Vol 4
Subject: Curative Education and Social Therapy

Karl König's collected works are issued by
the Karl König Archive, Aberdeen
in co-operation with the Ita Wegman Institute
for Basic Research into Anthroposophy, Arlesheim

Translated by Regina Erich

First published in German in 2008 under the title
Das Seelenpflege-bedürftige Kind by Verlag Freies Geistesleben
First published in English by Floris Books in 2009

British Library CIP Data available

ISBN 978-086315-693-9

Printed in Great Britain
by Bell & Bain, Glasgow

Contents

Curative Education, Modern Civilization and Social Community

The History and Future of Curative Education

Euthanasia

[We thought] that we could just adopt the existing name of the residential home chosen by our predecessor ... he was a doctor who had planned to establish a 'Home for Pathological and Epileptic Children.'

'No,' Dr Steiner replied, 'it needs to be seen already from the title what is happening there.'

I looked at him enquiringly whereupon he said: '*Curative and Educational Institute for Children in Need of Soul Care.*'

I still looked at him enquiringly, I didn't quite understand the new words but I pulled out my notebook and he dictated word by word ... And he added: 'We really need to choose a name which does not label the children right away.'

Albrecht Strohschein[1]

Die Ideale der Heilpädagogik
(für Heilpädagogen + solche die
es werden wollen.)

1) Die Geschichte der Heilpädagogik
2) Die Grundlagen der Heilpädagogik
3) Die Ziele der Heilpädagogik.

„Alles was ihr dem Geringsten
Meiner Brüder getan,
Das habt ihr Mir getan".

✝

Outline of König's planned book on the nature of curative education

Foreword

When Rudolf Steiner assisted Albrecht Strohschein, Siegfried Pickert and Franz Löffler in 1923/24 in establishing a curative-educational home based on anthroposophical principles he coined the term 'child in need of soul care.' Karl König (1902–66) who worked in curative education from 1927 onwards and who founded the Camphill movement in Scotland twelve years later kept to Rudolf Steiner's term which gave a valid name to the core task and aims of curative educational work. Georg von Arnim, König's student and co-worker, wrote in an essay by way of explanation:

> The term 'in need of soul care' is an expression for the *healing element in curative education*. Curative-educational interventions can *support the disturbed process of incarnation*, the efficacy of the child's emotional-spiritual energies can be enforced during his bodily development. Of course, in doing so you can sometimes achieve impressive progress whereas at other times there is hardly any visible success. But the essential thing is that a certain *development* actually *always* takes place which, however, cannot be rated in terms of 'normality' but of which it can be said: the body has developed into a slightly improved instrument. It gives the child's spiritual individuality the opportunity to have life experiences — which it is seeking and demanding — in a slightly more intense way. In the sense described here *healing* and *individualization* are *one and the same*.'[2]

For Karl König there were no 'pathological and epileptic children' but there were and are a lot of children 'in need' of an intense and specific support in their lives, a support described by Georg von Arnim as aiming to have effects on the physical existence. König's approach to curative education was an ethical-therapeutical one; he came across the children 'in need of soul care' during the course of his own life, and he gave them his unconditional support. As a student of Rudolf Steiner, König was convinced that the so-called handicapped people are integral human beings with an existing self, a human individuality, which in itself can neither be sick nor abnormal but which is of divine origin. In certain circumstances, however, this self may not fully incarnate in the body, the continuous permeation and materialization of which is a vital element of the life on earth. People 'in need of soul care' require intensive support and therapy in order to accomplish this task during their lives — an act which König had experienced earlier according to Jesus Christ's words, 'as you did it to one of the least of these my brethren, you did it to me.' (Matt.25:40).

Karl König's medical work at anthroposophical curative-educational institutes started in 1927 at the Sonnenhof in Arlesheim and continued from summer 1928 at Pilgramshain, near Breslau (now Wroclaw in Poland). From the start it was meant to be a co-operative one. The collaborative aspect of supporting children in need of soul care was of extraordinary importance to König: he considered this as the approach towards a future civilization based on humanitarian values. When König and his young friends fled from the National Socialists in 1938/39 to Scotland the co-operative dimension of his efforts grew further. Against the background of the distant war in Central Europe the future Camphill movement took shape. It was an international impulse of peace and therapy based on the anthroposophical image of the human being. Three years after the end of the war he wrote about what had been achieved and the further aims:

We now care for and educate 180 children, and if we had more space we could accommodate double the number without difficulty. The children hail from Scotland, England and the colonies — from South Africa, India, Kenya, Ceylon — so that a large group from far and wide, bound by destiny, has come together here. The teachers and nurses, doctors and helpers, more than sixty in number, form another branch of this network of destiny. They come from Scotland, England, Ireland, Austria and Germany, from Bohemia, Holland, from Switzerland and Sweden. Together, in this special, sacred land, we are attempting to create an environment that is appropriate for these children with special needs. They learn to work in the garden, to plough the fields, to sow seeds, to weave and spin in the workshops, to cut wood and to carve it. In the kitchens they learn to cook and in their homes they must learn to do normal housework. They learn to sing and make music, to do eurythmy, to play the lyre. But many must first learn to listen, to speak, to walk, to think. But the co-workers are aware that the children can only learn when they, the teachers, are prepared to educate themselves; therefore, in a truly social community we learn to live with each other and fruitfully integrate our personality into the larger social context. Self-education is only possible when all members of the community share a common ideal.

For that reason the training here at Camphill focuses on the image of the human being; the star we are aspiring to reach is the 'human image' in its physical, soul and spiritual form. We believe that if we are able to light up the true image of a human being in our hearts, we help all those children in whom this human image reveals itself in a distorted or deformed way. So we inwardly uphold what can be of constant support and healing to the children. They not only need appropriate education and support, not only the necessary medicines, not only artistic activity and the possibility to do work that is useful to the world — these children need a community of educators and nurses, doctors and helpers who inwardly uphold what the children lack: the true image of the human being.

Through this practice, therapeutic education — in the way that it is being attempted here — will become a crucial social issue, as is already becoming a reality in Scotland. 'Because the social question is essentially an education question, and the education question is essentially a medical question — but only for the kind of medicine that has been made fruitful by spiritual science.' These words, spoken by Rudolf Steiner on April 7, 1920 at the Goetheanum, show that questions of medicine, education and the social life form a unity which can first be realized in caring for children who are outcasts from society. They bear the future within themselves.[3]

Alfred Heidenreich, a priest of the Christian Community who had visited König in Camphill during the Second World War later recalled:

In the summer of 1941 I spent two months in the Dee Valley to recover from a severe illness. Soon I called at Camphill nearly every other day. It was a time for conversations while far away the war took its inexorable course. König expounded his vision of the future. Deep and genuine, constructive and understanding as his devotion was to 'children in need of special care,' he explained that his curative work was not entirely an end in itself but also a means to establish residential communities, in the spirit of Rudolf Steiner's teaching.

One day they might become islands in which the life of
the spirit can survive, when wave after wave of
catastrophes will engulf humanity towards the end of the
century. He thought that these 'backward' children had a
mission to bring people together in communities even as
they had a mission to awaken special love and
compassion in their parents and other members of their
families.[4]

Karl König tried all his life to work for curative education on
a grand scale, established countless contacts and, as a cosmopoli-
tan, encouraged the Camphill foundations to be open to the
world. He was serious about the cultural tasks of those new
communities which form around people in need of soul care in
curative-educational workplaces, as well as communal living and
also within the children's families.

In my opinion, the more our understanding of the true
nature of the 'special care' child grows, the fewer
institutions and residential special schools will be needed
for such children. I regard these arrangements as an
unavoidable transitional stage, necessary until we
physicians as well as the teachers and especially the
parents once more realize that the family is the proper
place for each of these children. It is there and nowhere
else that they, like all children, are 'at home.'[5]

König regarded the increase of (at first glance) 'handicapped' persons, but also after 1945 the awakening social conscience for them, as a pointer towards the future. He was
fully convinced that the incidence of people 'in need of soul
care' is correlated with the living conditions in a highly tech-
nological civilization and its imminent decline of social stan-
dards, but at the same time it offers the opportunity of
redirecting this development towards a newly arising humanity. In many ways König experienced the 'handicapped' as

educators of the 'normal' people, at least in the sense of a *mutual* relationship. König not only developed numerous innovative ways of diagnosis and therapy in and together with Camphill but he also wanted to raise the social awareness of curative education as a special task of our time during an era of extremes which not only brought, as Asperger said, the 'endangerment of the individual human being as well as the social community,' but the actual 'approval of the annihilation of life unworthy of living.'[6] Within this dramatic ongoing situation, König laid the foundations of his curative-educational work based on anthroposophy. In one of his lecture manuscripts König wrote: 'What can we do? Curative education is full well the task of the curative teacher but it is also a precept for *all* people. Because it is about a change of attitude so that justice is done to these children. They are not at all to be pitied but to be admired. And we need to learn step by step to understand this.'[7]

In his essay 'The Problem of Euthanasia,' subtitled 'A Word About Catel's Disastrous Book,' which König published in 1963 in the journal *Die Drei,* he quoted Rudolf Steiner:

> There is something today, which is just at its very beginning, which, however, is able to reveal great understanding of human nature: the observation of so-called pathological individuals. To observe what could in a philistine way be called a 'not normal' person awakens a feeling, you can become one with this person, with this person you can deepen your self-understanding, you can go further when you get under his skin ... But you have to develop a sense for this observation, and not allow yourself to be repulsed by it. You really have to tell yourself that sometimes the tragic things in life, however unwished for, are the ones that can open the deepest secrets of life ... That is the 'school of interest in other people.' In other words,

the world comes towards us with the hardship of illness in order to hold our interest, and the interest in the other is what socially will bring humankind forward in the time to come.[8]

Werner Catel (1894–1981) had sent König his book on the problem of limited euthanasia *Grenzsituationen des Lebens: Beitrag zum Problem einer begrenzten Euthanasie,* published in 1962 with 'deep respect and solidarity' ('because he expected that I would make my opinion of it known'[9]). Since 1933 — after his Jewish predecessor's removal from office — Catel had been professor for neurology and psychiatry and director of the pediatric clinic at the University in Leipzig. In a leading position he had contributed to the euthanasia programme of the National Socialists. Under his guidance more than 500 children had been killed in children's specialist departments. Despite this he had managed to continue his academic career in West Germany after the end of the Second World War and to become professor for pediatrics at the University of Kiel in 1954 before he had to take early retirement following increasing public pressure.[10] In this book, Catel — who denied having had any part in what had happened during the Third Reich — still promoted a 'limited euthanasia' for 'humanitarian' reasons in cases of 'completely imbecile children' who were incapable of any social contact: 'An imbecile child is ... a creature on a level far below the existence of an animal with a soul and which vegetates as a creature with no faculty of reason, without any mental activity, as a *massa carnis.'*[11] In König's profound and detailed criticism of Catel's book, he again extensively examined the concept of deficiency:

> Could it not be that especially those who are disabled and weak, crippled and abnormal *direct* us towards the way to the light? Why do they have to be rated as mentally deficient and worthless? Is not the temptation

of the idea of usefulness already taking effect when coming to such conclusions? Only one small step further and the teachings about the 'approval of the annihilation of unworthy life' propagated by Hoche and Binding will be taken up again. Catchphrases like 'reason of state' and 'space for the efficient ones' will reveal their double face and once again people will start looking for 'sensible and efficient solutions' for an ever-increasing population. As long as 'cripples' — whether mental or physical — are rated by us as inferior human beings, no barrier of clear insight will stand against such actions. The problem of euthanasia will always be about the *renewal of the idea of humanity*.'[12]

König saw the risks of a bioethical and social-economical way of thinking in the field of medicine. These risks had not ceased with the end of National Socialism but continued to be of influence, and together with medical-technical procedures continually created new challenges (for example in the field of prenatal diagnostics and interventions). König not only advocated the right to life of each human being and saw the greater purpose of troubled lives (in the sense of the idea of incarnation and reincarnation) but also encouraged the quality of creating and maintaining individual relationships. He wrote in opposition to Catel and following the quote of Rudolf Steiner about the 'school of interest in other people':

Here the path is shown which alone can lead to overcoming all misconceptions of euthanasia. The human interest in another human being, and the experience which needs to become an everyday experience for the curative teacher: that he has the opportunity to truly encounter the image of the human being in the 'pathological' or 'abnormal' child. For there something begins to be revealed that in a normal person (if such a person exists at all) appears to be still veiled.

This is what is disastrous about Catel's book, that he pities aberration, that he wants to feel sorry for it and — as a 'normal person' — feels painfully called upon to be a judge for euthanasia. Not only is this a lack of understanding but cheap sentimentality. No abnormal child seeks help and protection. What they demand is understanding and acknowledgment. They all are aware of their own humanity and even a *massa carnis* (to use Luther's phrase) is enveloped in the veil of the soul and the shine of an individual spirit. If communication with other people cannot be achieved then it will be similar to what Lichtenberg said about books: 'If a head and a book bump into each other and there is a hollow sound then this is not always caused by the book.' Whoever seeks contact with these people and turns to them on an equal footing will never fail to establish communication, for they will always hear and answer a genuine call.[13]

★

This volume of the Karl König Archive collected works combines lectures, manuscripts and essays of Karl König which focus on the nature of curative education — its historical background and substantial challenges, its social and ethical implication and purpose. König spoke in many countries about the child 'in need of soul care' and the curative education practised in Camphill. He spoke out of the depths of his experience, with an impressive heart knowledge and as one whose life's work was far-reaching. König spoke to specialists, scientists, self-help organizations, parents and affected people, and he contributed to various journals and anthologies. As early as February 1945 he planned to write an introductory book about the nature of curative education which he wanted to name *The Ideals of Curative Education,* which was to consist of three parts:

1. History of Curative Education
2. Principles of Curative Education
3. Aims of Curative Education.'[14]

Sadly König's introductory book never came into being, but the lectures and essays in this volume are in line with his intentions of 1945.

The printed text has had only minor revisions, updating some of the terms for illnesses used by König (for example, for Down's syndrome he used the term 'mongolism' introduced by John Langdon-Down in 1866). The references in the texts are König's. The collection is preceded by an introductory article by Georg von Arnim which was published soon after Dr König's death. Studies on special curative eduction, diagnostics, nosology (the classification of diseases), and therapy are planned.

Peter Selg
Ita Wegman Institute
Arlesheim, July 2008

Introduction

Karl König —
Curative Teacher and Physician

Georg von Arnim

Karl König went across the threshold of death into the spiritual world, out of a life of the richest activity, full of plans and new intentions. Among these were a number of lectures already scheduled for several occasions.

It falls to the author of these lines in the hour of such a planned lecture which Dr König could not hold himself, to say a few words about him.

These attempts to speak about him, to describe important features of his life, are associated with an impressive experience of seeing from how many sides such a portrayal is possible. What manifoldness lived and came to expression in Karl König. How all the forces and possibilities of his life in their deepest aspects existed in mutual balance. The important Christian personality, the pupil of Rudolf Steiner, the doctor of embryology, the curative teacher, the social researcher, the writer and lecturer. And above all, the brother and man of our time, the man of this twentieth century, which is thrown hither and thither by such apocalyptic upheavals.

He was in the highest sense a bearer and shaper of the

twentieth century. A personality with great strength of cultural expression, with deep care and interest for the human being — even more for the child as it is thrown into the storms of this time.

So he stood in our world of abstraction and ideologies, of theories and theses, of mass culture and withdrawal. And he unfolded thereby in special ways a quality which, healing and helping and so bitterly needed, wanted to live in just this world. He stood there, as we already said, as a pupil of Rudolf Steiner, and he stood surrounded and united, leading and led by a human community.

Against this background could appear his quite extraordinary capacity for imaginative experiences, and also for imaginative pictorial expression and writing.

In this way much was revealed to him which is not available to a categorized thinking which only measures and counts. This is not the place to speak about imaginative thinking and experience, or about being imaginative in our time. But one may be allowed to say that it was through this capacity that Karl König stood in the world as he did. It opened to him an unusual, immediate and direct entry to so many other human souls. It brought about his ability to master problems of contact, of communication in a way which really only in our time can be shown to be modern and fitting. He easily made a very deep impression on everyone whom he met and with whom he spoke. It always happened that when he thought about the other person, a living picture came before his soul of the personality of the human being whom he had met. This brought about a mutual sphere of meeting which encourages and creates human contact.

Karl König belonged to the important curative teachers, recognized and respected both publicly and by the international professional world. His influence on a very wide public regarding the position and direction of the needs and problems of handicapped children, young people and adults, will only be realized in its future development.

However, the aspect of his personality as a physician did not appear as clearly in the eyes of the world. Something about this side of his being will therefore be said here.

Physician and curative teacher had an intimate and significant relationship in the person of Karl König. When he had to act he let medical wisdom — not only knowledge but deepest wisdom — flow into his curative intentions. And in the manner of his medical dealings there unfolded an element taken from the sphere of curative education. While in the medical side of his personality he distilled in a number of curative therapies, so on the other hand the curative teacher in him worked towards the essential form and furtherance of the relationship between the doctor and his patients, between man as healer and man as sufferer.

It is just this relationship which is more and more challenged in our time of increasing rationalization and technicality of all medical dealings, as much from the side of the patients as from that of the doctor. The natural certainty and immediacy of earlier times no longer shows itself in this relationship. A great social problem is being enacted here before our eyes. The most manifold considerations will be given to it, to what lies at its basis, and to how one can guide this development. So it may be allowed, with the eyes of a doctor to contemplate the important and basic contribution which Karl König has made to the problem through the manner in which he united medical and curative educational activity in himself. It is unimportant that this concerns an area which did not stand so strongly in the foreground. It lay continually at Karl König's heart.

What is it really which seemed to lead the development of the relationship between the doctor and his patients into quite new lines? Why is it that the intimate relation which existed between the old family doctor and his patients no longer comes about? It is a retrogressive movement which increasingly loses the capacity to see the individuality of the person, to see his uniqueness. And this is within a medicine oriented more and more to rationalization, statistical evaluations and so-called negative proof. At the same time there is a noticeable loss of the person himself in his spiritual meaning. Dr König concerned himself intensively and most carefully with this matter, for instance in the article about man and his future.[1] This whole development is characterized by the most feeble attempts to truly behold the spirit of another human being, and to be able to encounter the spiritual individuality in him.

But it is just this ability that is the innermost demand of curative education. We mentioned how greatly Dr König had this faculty at his disposal. If one could count them all, there was an unbelievable number of people towards whom he showed it — sick and healthy, handicapped and normal, children and adults. To this must be added something else, namely his tremendous interest in studying the human constitution. Already well qualified by his work in embryology, it came easily to him to distinguish the constitutional similarities between particular groups of the many children whom he treated.

Thus there has come to us the imaginative knowledge of constitutional gestalt, of forms, which is not content with a mere enumeration of particular symptoms. He could discover so much of the history of human development because he saw it against the background of Rudolf Steiner's teaching.

But he did not stop at the consideration of common constitutional characteristics. He invariably sought for each visiting child knowledge of that individual and their special, personal destiny. His interpretation and description of Down's syndrome is indicative of this kind of insight into constitutionally similar groups as regards their purpose within human development. But sentences such as the following are decisive in the way they point towards the individual:

> Despite the similarity which Down's syndrome gives to its bearer, they show a great manifoldness. Therefore one must not confuse the individual uniqueness of the

Down's syndrome child with the broad variations of the Down's syndrome child. Down's syndrome is a symptom in a human being, but the human being is more than the Down's syndrome with which he is permeated. And it is not easy, to gradually learn to distinguish the one from the other. In any case they must be differentiated, the individuality and his Down's syndrome.[2]

Thus there are two opposite tendencies, clearly distinct. It is this first tendency, coming from many streams of our time, to take less and less note of the single individual, to overwhelm it with statistical abstractions thus making it meaningless. The result of this development appears in medical practice, and has its consequences especially in the doctor-patient relationship.

All this Karl König felt in the deepest sense and he experienced it as a clear 'threat to the person.' Thus he formulated it in his last essay about the inner importance and nature of curative education. To fight against this threat to the person is the nature and task of the 'curative educational attitude.'

Karl König gave a wonderful description of this attitude in which he said:

Only support from person to person — the encounter of a self with another self— the awareness of another individuality without questioning the other's religion, convictions and political background — just the gaze from eye to eye between two personalities, creates the kind of curative education which can, in a healing way, counteract the threat to the core of humanity.[3]

And suddenly, what was thus begun is led to a decisive climax. To a saying which can only be seen as the fruit of ripest humanity and as a legacy:

> Above all, however, curative education is not only
> science, not only practical art but a *human attitude*. But as
> such it can be given like a healing remedy to those who
> are under the devastating threat to the human
> personality. This, however, is the fate of every human
> being today. It is in resisting this, in helping and
> receiving help, that the meaning and the value of
> curative-educational work lies.[4]

The way in which Karl König united the medical and the curative educational in his person, takes a special place in our time. It was possible for him, thanks to his facility with pictures and forms, to take up the nature and meaning of all that he encountered, especially of each person he met, in the most immediate way. With this union which he carried within himself, he was able to administer to medicine itself a 'healing medicine.'

I want to conclude with some words of Max Scheler, a German philosopher whom Karl König deeply respected. In his treatment of the 'sense of suffering' he speaks about 'the undoubtedly increasing suffering of the growing civilization and culture.' This was said less than half a century ago. The development since then has in many respects gone far beyond what Scheler could foresee. The following that he added endures so much more:

> It is the joy of growing love, the extensively and
> intensively growing community of life with its historic
> qualities which must compensate and, finally, even more
> than compensate, for the increasing pain attendant to
> such growth.[5]

This 'growing love' for mankind, wherever and in whichever form he encountered it, lived in Karl König.

To Parents

THE HANDICAPPED CHILD

LETTERS TO PARENTS

I

Dr. KARL KÖNIG

The title page of Karl König's publication of 1964.

1

Letter to the Parents
of Camphill at
Lake Constance

Dear Parents,

To my great regret it is unfortunately not possible for me to be personally present at your gathering, to greet you, to speak with you and also tell you something of the thoughts and feelings which I cherish on such a day.

But you will excuse my absence in the knowledge that I am ill at present and therefore unable to speak to you. It is difficult to write what I would dearly like to have said because the human contact which otherwise carries and aids the speaker is now lacking.

What I wanted to express would have been along these lines: that you as parents try to unite yourselves more and more with the work that we are doing here. Not only because we are doing it for your children but because it is happening to all. For in being together with handicapped, retarded and emotionally disturbed people there arises a new image of true humanity. And it is not the teachers, houseparents, helpers and doctors who create this image; they merely endeavour to make it visible, so that — in Goethe's words — it becomes an open secret. It is created solely by the children who have been entrusted to you and to us: you as parents, we as educators in the widest sense.

We should all be increasingly filled with the idea that these children are our teachers; teachers in a higher sense. For they have taken their destiny — to be bent and deformed, ill prepared for life and retarded — upon themselves. They do not complain and are not surly. They also do not accuse or bewail their fate. Rather do they take their being different courageously upon themselves, in the way that a person carries his cross on his shoulders, and says 'yes' to it, unreservedly.

We should not think that they do not understand who and how they are. They know this very well and nevertheless remain courageous, cheerful and full of hope. Should we not follow their example? All of us? Which of us does not let our courage fail and our hope wane more often than our children? It is in this sense that I mean they are our teachers.

But also in another sense. Each of our children contributes to the winning of a great battle which has been fought by people for thousands of years. The whole of history, in all its sufferings, deeds and achievements, is an expression of this battle. It is the ongoing battle that the spirit wages against the needs of the body. That body which since the Fall has been ensnared and penetrated by our souls. The spirit of each person's individuality lighting up in his soul tries ever and again to free itself from the bondage of sin. If the body is healthy, we succumb all too easily to its drives, desires and longings. But if it is ailing and infirm, it reminds us of the hardships and troubles of existence.

That is what our children constantly bring home to us. They show us the other side of life, which is just as necessary and important as that in which we are immersed every day. Here too our children are our teachers. They help us — through their daily appearance, through their hardships and tribulations — to keep the spiritual spark of our soul awake and not to forget the oil in our lamps. Our children are not warriors but gentle, though constant admonishers in the great battle of the history of humankind.

What would we do without them? Would not the whole of humanity lose its social balance if sorrow and pain, difference and specialness were not to appear constantly before us? Only superficial people could be of the opinion that the world should exist without illness and need. If this were so, how would we know what joy or a sense of gladness is? Is not the love that rules over everything both pain and joy? Is not grace both challenge and conquest? Is not faith both doubt and blessedness?

In such moments we want to remember this. We want to say a full unreserved 'yes' to our children and to their and our destiny, to this difficult task. Only this 'yes' gives our children the true foundation on which they can stand and live. Only such a 'yes' gives them the solidity of their and our existence.

For only then do we reaffirm the words Christ spoke to his disciples, that those alone are blessed who are sorrowful. They shall be comforted, but in being comforted they will give still greater comfort.

Such thoughts can unite us as parents and educators. Our children are not there merely so that we may help them; they are there so that we may be helped through them.

It is a mutual giving and taking. A power can arise from this which has become so rare today, which we all seem to be losing and is nevertheless so important in human communication — trust.

Trust in the other person.

Trust in the divine world.

Rudolf Steiner was once asked what is needed in the modern world. He answered, 'To base our lives on simple trust, without security of existence, to have trust in the ever-present help of the spiritual world.'

This we can learn every day anew from our children, and we want to try never to forget it.

This is what I wanted to say to you, dear parents, as a greeting and as a guide in your initiatives.

Yours,
Dr König

Brachenreuthe, May 1, 1965

2

To the Mother
of a Down's Syndrome Child

Dear Mrs Elderly,

I was very sorry indeed that you were unable to accompany Timothy when he came to see me a few days ago. Your husband, however, was able to tell me a good deal of Timothy's history, and it was therefore possible to obtain a full picture of the child's past and present condition. Mr Elderly asked me to write to you in detail about Timothy, and also to let you have my advice on his further education and upbringing.

The problem concerning your child is not a simple one. First of all you should know that there are thousands of mothers in this country who have similar children. I understand that you are aware that your little son is classified as having Down's syndrome, and as he is nearly five years old, his further training is now the main problem. You have been given very varying views by the specialists whom you have consulted so far, but they were all agreed upon the diagnosis.

Let me say to begin with that a Down's syndrome child is not a mentally defective child and that, though Timothy definitely has Down's syndrome, he is already able to walk and to make himself understood in simple words and, therefore, can be more easily trained than many Down's syndrome children. He is lively, active, has a good sense of humour and is an excellent mixer. Everybody who meets him is fond of him and his memory is exceptionally good. He loves music, and can repeat almost immediately any tune he has heard. All this shows that he is a child who has qualities of mind and heart which many other children lack.

On the other hand, you have already encountered some of his difficulties which are very typical of Down's syndrome. Your husband especially referred to his stubbornness, and to his inability to obey. If he has set his mind on a thing it is not easy to distract him, but if this should happen he may become sulky for a short time. This attitude has a very simple root in all Down's syndrome children as every one of them is exceedingly bashful, and their sense of shame is so strong that it appears as stubbornness. I would advise you to take this into consideration. If he becomes obstinate, turn away from him and speak to him in a low voice in order to let him know that you understand this feeling of shame.

His inability to obey is due to his great lack of understanding of what we consider to be right and wrong, and here we meet one of the fundamental characteristics of a Down's syndrome person. He belongs to that type of human being who is so child-like in all his habits, that our ordinary code of good and evil is not applicable. Down's syndrome people live in a world of equal values, where everybody is good, and everything is nice and agreeable. Therefore they are innately happy, and only very few of them show a streak of cruelty or bad temper. For this reason they hardly ever develop what is usually termed 'conscience,' and they will always retain a happy-go-lucky character.

This, of course, will in turn bring certain deficiencies, but these will only make their appearance in Timothy at some time in the future. He will never be able to think in the form of abstract ideas. Therefore you must expect that, for him, arithmetic will always remain a realm into which he cannot enter. He may learn to count and do simple addition and subtraction, but this will be done more as a kind of repetition than with any real understanding. Nevertheless he will certainly be able to learn to read and write, if special instruction can be started not later than his seventh nor earlier than his sixth year.

He is not likely to be able to write a proper essay, nor will he enjoy reading books which need much thought, but he should have a good deal of education as he will greatly enjoy being taught all kinds of subjects, such as painting, singing, history of humankind, botany, zoology, etc.

I would not advise you to send him to a residential home or institution, but to keep him with you for as long as possible. It would be good for him to attend a nursery class, and later you should try to find a small private school where there would be some understanding for his shortcomings. So long as he is with you in the company of his older brothers and sisters, he will be a source of joy and happiness to you all.

If however you are unable to find an appropriate day school for him I shall be willing to advise you about a residential school where he can be suitably educated and spend his holidays at home.

Timothy is not a burden but just the opposite. He is a grace which has been bestowed on you and your family, because through him you will learn that the real values of human life do not lie in intellectual capacities only, but in the depths of the human soul. Is he not a better person than most of us? Are his qualities of heart not greater than those of most other children? Why should we not take account of his loving attitude and carefree mind? Is it not a blessing to have children like him among us?

You will agree that this is right, but you will ask what will become of him, when his parents have gone? This, of course, is a serious problem and cannot easily be answered. Don't you think that for all our children the question is the same nowadays, and that we are asking ourselves what will become of them if the present social conditions prevail? Timothy will certainly not be called up, should another world war threaten our whole civilization, but what may otherwise confront him? I am convinced that he rests in the hands of God, at least as much as any other human being; and should you not develop an attitude of faith and trust for his future? There are still to be found many good souls who are willing to help if need be. In ten or fifteen years this country may have awakened to the needs of these children. By that time, there will perhaps exist places where love and understanding have helped to build villages for such human beings.

Timothy will be able to learn a simple trade and thereby earn his living if guided and helped in an appropriate way. At the moment let us simply consider his present training and education, and at some time to come we might discuss his future in more detail.

I hope this will help you to understand your child. Should you have any further questions I shall be only too glad to answer them.

Yours sincerely,
Karl König

The Task and Ethics of
Curative Education

3

The Purpose and Value of Curative-Educational Work

1

Curative education, as it is called today, identifies and describes a relatively new field of human activity — in contrast to *curative science* which from the very beginnings of civilization accompanied the development of the human mind as a profession and vocation. From the earliest days of humankind there were physicians, priests and priest doctors; but no curative educators until very recently.

It is not easy to detect the historical beginnings of curative-educational work. Its earliest roots are embedded in medical ground. The well-known physician, Paracelsus (1494–1541) was the first who pointed out the connection between struma and mental deficiency. Also at the same time the first real attempts were made to teach and educate blind and deaf-mute children (Ponce, Ammann).

But not until the eighteenth century was the actual breakthrough brought about. Specific curative-educational work first originated in France, shortly after that in Switzerland and also in Germany. In Paris, Abbé de l'Epée attended to the needs of deaf-mute people and in 1770 he founded the first institute for hearing-impaired children and young people. A few years later — in 1778 — Samuel Heinicke established a similar school in Leipzig. Almost simultaneously the first educational institutes for the blind were founded by Valentin Haüy in Paris, Berlin and Petersburg.

At the end of the same century Itard and Séguin, both French, facilitated the actual inauguration of curative education. Itard looked after a feral child who had been found by hunters in one of the forests of Aveyron. He wanted to re-humanize the child but was only partly successful. The effort and work he put into this child kindled in him the impulse to generally teach and educate people with mental deficiencies, and in this way he opened departments for mentally deficient children and young people within the two — by then already famous — mental hospitals in Paris, the Bicétre and Salpétiere. Together with Ferrus and Bourneville, Itard founded the science of curative education. Séguin became his student who brought the new impulse to North America. There — in New York and in Massachusetts — curative-educational homes were established.

In Switzerland, Pestalozzi was the first who attended to the needs of neglected and orphaned children and who wanted to raise them to become human beings in the best possible way. And two decades later the young medical student Johann Jacob Guggenbühl — while on a walk in the Alps — took the decision to support mentally deficient children in a way that would allow their ability to learn and work to be kindled.

Around 1840 he founded the then much noted and admired Institution for Cretins on the Abendberg near Interlaken. There he tried to manage — often without fully appropriate means and sufficient stamina — a curative-educational residential home which was a school at the same time.

At this time everywhere in Europe similar institutions came into existence. The fate of those who were mentally deficient, developmentally retarded, imbecile, poor and neglected came more and more into the focus of the social conscience of the civilized nations. And we must not ignore the fact that the awakening of a scientific and practical curative education is closely linked to the social changes during that era.

In Paris, in the midst of the fighting and events of the French Revolution, the first curative-educational beginnings came into existence. In Stans and Burgdorf, Pestalozzi gathered the children who had been stranded on the shores of life by the gory waves of this revolution. Those who had been deemed victims by the rage of misconceived social ideals were offered a newly arising humanity by healing hands.

Whether afflictions had been caused by disease, injury, abnormality, neglect or disregard — all of a sudden they came into the focus of individual people who recognized the distress and misery of these children. Curative education was no longer restricted to the mental deficiency of developmentally retarded children. It established itself also in situations where children were bound to deteriorate because of social deprivation, poverty and incapability, misery and ignorance. For this reason reformers like Thomas Barnardo and Don Bosco — founders of schools, educational institutions and training centres for orphaned children — are as much curative educators as Itard, Séguin, Pestalozzi and Guggenbühl. Here a wide subject came into being which has been accessible to humankind only for the last two hundred years.

2

But what is curative education? There have been numerous attempts to describe, or even to define, the concept of curative education.[1] The great philosopher and educator Eduard Spranger said: 'Education should steer body and soul through the process of growth in a healthy way. Curative education is specifically tasked to heal that which has fallen ill.' Theodor Heller, the great Austrian veteran of curative education at the beginning of the twentieth century, said:

> Curative education's field includes all those mental
> abnormalities occurring during childhood whose

psychological dysfunctions can be restored by creating supportive developmental conditions that need to be adjusted to each individual case. Not just mental disorders but also disorders of the emotions and the will require curative-educational treatment.

And the author of the first truly comprehensive textbook of curative education, August Homburger, wrote:

Curative education is the combination of education and teaching with interventions which aim to heal, improve and compensate mental health deficiencies. All curative education is based on the fact that there are mental irregularities of various kinds and degrees which require educational and teaching interventions other than those long established and modified.[2]

Since these statements were made, the situation of curative education has undergone vast change. From the periphery of education, pediatrics and psychiatry, it has shifted into the focus of many teachers, doctors, social workers, psychologists and psychiatrists. The extensive field of child psychiatry is in the process of developing and in every part of the civilized world there are efforts in curative education. In a lecture during the therapy week in Karlsruhe in 1958, I defined curative education as the 'practice and application of insights gained from child psychiatry.'

And in the introduction to his textbook published more than ten years ago Hans Asperger, pediatrician and curative teacher, wrote words which still apply today:

We will call curative education the science which, based on a biological knowledge of abnormal child personalities, aims to find mainly educational ways to treat cognitive and sensory deficiencies, and mental and emotional disorders during childhood and youth. The best human guidance resulting from an understanding of the human being can, so we think, influence disturbed personalities in a positive way.[3]

And he justifiably added:

This work — whether it is called 'curative education' or a different name — has most recently experienced an enormous upturn because it has been recognized that its aims arise from a particularly urgent concern regarding our current situation. Without a doubt this is associated with the threat that at present looms over cultural life as a whole and affects individual human beings as well as society.

You could not find a clearer and better description of the special task of curative education today. The earlier definitions above were still abstract and academic. But here the true task of curative education as a requirement arising from prevailing circumstances becomes most evident. This kind of work only gains justification today because human beings — whether children or adults — increasingly find themselves in a special situation in which they need direction, guidance and support.

An affluent society that is about to forget its humanity; a society that becomes deeply involved in its racial problems and at the same time has made weapons that can destroy millions of people in a few minutes; a society that has forgotten the divine order is seeking new ethics which it cannot find in a state of godlessness; such a society brings about a new set of tasks: to support those who are disabled, timid, lame and ailing in such a way that they can reclaim their humanity.

Is it not a great miracle that wants to manifest itself here? A self-destructive humanity creates within itself something new like a fresh bud within the dying part of its existence. A comprehensive curative education is like the developing seed inside a rotting fruit.

We only need to define the concept of curative education widely enough to see its true purpose. It is more than just practical child psychiatry and educational and psychological efforts to handle maladjusted children and dropped out young people. Its intention is to become a global task to help counteract the 'threat to the individual person' which has arisen everywhere. The 'curative-educational attitude' needs to express itself in any social work, in pastoral care, in the care for the elderly, in the rehabilitation of mentally ill and physically handicapped people, in the guidance of orphans and refugees, of suicidal and desperate individuals, in the international Peace Corps and similar ambitions.

This is the only answer we have today — inasmuch as we still want to be human beings — for a society dancing on the brink of disaster. No philosophy congresses, international conferences, religious gatherings and enormous scientific events will influence this dance of death in any way. On these occasions everybody just wants to hear themselves and — while staying within the rules — bring attention to themselves.

Only support from person to person — the encounter of a self with another self — the awareness of another individuality without questioning the other's religion, convictions and political background — just the gaze from eye to eye between two personalities, creates the kind of curative education which can, in a healing way, counteract the threat to the core of humanity.

However, this can only work on the strength of profound heart-knowledge.

3

This vital insight is not easy to gain and even more difficult to put into practice, because it is associated with one's own personality and work in the light of self-assessment. What I mean is this: we need to learn to see ourselves as creative educators in such a way that we are not only the leaders, but at the same time those who are being led; not just the teachers but students at the same time. As long as the patient is only being assessed by the doctor and the latter does not see himself as a patient in the light of the illness, he remains a quack and charlatan.

How many psychologists and psychotherapists regard their patients as grass and weed without realizing that they themselves — even if they have undergone a training in analysis — are not flowers but part of the grass?

Curative teachers and social workers often consider themselves superior to children and parents. When encountering those who are physically and mentally disabled, who seek help and ask for guidance, it is all too easy to conduct oneself as the more capable one.

The curative-educational attitude only develops if a new sense of humility begins to grow in one's heart which recognizes the brother in every human face. A humility which is so steadfast and yet so gentle that it fills our eyes with tears in the face of misery, humiliation and suffering — tears which make us strong and resolved in our intention to devote ourselves to help. That is what it is about.

Such tears make us immediately understand that I can only help if I am intent to see the helper in the brother and in myself the one who receives help. If I help him, I will be helped. If I guide him, he will lead me. If I feed him, I will be given bread myself. Only then will the words of the Gospel become a reality, 'as you did it to one of the least of these my brethren, you did it to me' (Matt.25:40).

Curative education was and is a developing science; as such it belongs to the field of child psychiatry and has a part in pediatrics, neurology and psychology.

But it is also a practical art which develops ever further. As such it has a part in pedagogics, special needs education in schools and in many more fields than these. Logopaedics, physiotherapy, eurythmy and curative eurythmy, pedagogical painting, drawing and playing music, music and speech therapy belong to it as well as all craft activities like weaving, pottery, carving and all kinds of so-called occupational therapy.

Above all, however, curative education is not only science, not only practical art, but a *human attitude*. But as such it can be given like a healing remedy to those who are under the devastating threat to the human personality. This, however, is the fate of every human being today. It is in resisting this, in helping and receiving help, that the meaning and the value of curative-educational work lies.

4

The Care and Education
of Handicapped Children

In the following, I wish to present a survey of the care and education of handicapped children gained from thirty years' experience in this field. I not only want to describe the specialized teaching of educationally subnormal children, nor will I confine myself to the special care of maladjusted and socially deranged children, but I wish to include all aspects of the management and thereby the practice of those conditions which are described by modern child psychiatry.

Amongst the sciences the practice and theory of child psychiatry is a very young branch. I do not think that its real beginnings were earlier than twenty-five years ago. Before this there were only a few outstanding personalities who devoted themselves to children in need of special care and whom we credit with great and valuable achievements within their limited possibilities. To make myself understood, I need only point to men like Itard, Séguin, Pestalozzi, Guggenbühl and Theodor Heller. In their time, the great curative teacher had to be all in one. He had to diagnose the children's condition, care for them, be their teacher and their father-image.

During the course of the Second World War, and particularly since its conclusion, the conscience of civilized humankind has been aroused by the backward and handicapped child (the child in need of special care) and since that time we have been able to witness a great advance in child psychiatry, especially in the western world. Thus in Britain in the last fifteen years, many day schools, occupation centres and residential schools have been opened by the authorities, and groups of children are being educated and treated in quite an exemplary way. Similar efforts are being made in America, Switzerland and other countries. Most significant, however, is that the general public is becoming aware of the problems of the mentally handicapped child to an extent hitherto unknown. No longer does one regard these children as human outcasts, fit only to be put away in some home so that they should not be a public nuisance; and no longer do parents hide them because they feel ashamed of them, but they are looked upon as sick human beings who, like all other children, have a right to be educated and to be given the appropriate treatment. The atmosphere of the poorhouse and of the public institution that had so long been the stigma of these children is gradually being dispelled.

We shall now try to distinguish various components of the practice of child psychiatry. In my opinion these can be divided into four principal sections:

1. Diagnosis
2. Treatment
3. Education
4. Care

In practice, these are not four watertight compartments, but they overlap and should work together and concurrently. Yet they have to be distinguished so that the structure and pattern of practical child psychiatry can become clear. I shall begin by speaking about these sections singly and then try to deal with the subject as a whole.

1. Diagnosis

Only a beginning has been made here as with the rest of child psychiatry. In fact, scientifically based care and education only start when a comprehensive diagnosis is attempted, that is, when we avoid the fundamental mistake of labelling children as feeble-minded, imbecile, etc., and then believe we have arrived at a proper diagnosis. I must emphasize most strongly that these categories which are still in use convey nothing whatever about the nature of a mentally handicapped child. They are unscientific terms and at best a classification for legal purposes, of concern to the physician and teacher only on particular occasions.

Feeble-mindedness, imbecility and idiocy are the outcome of complicated processes that have to be carefully discerned prior to considering any such diagnosis. To this end we should harness all the resources of modern neurology, psychiatry and psychology. Even then we shall often be faced with an unsolved problem and only in time may this yield to a multilateral diagnostic approach. Whenever we are concerned with a backward or handicapped child, we should not be content with antiquated terms such as 'retardation' or 'congenital mental deficiency.' From my own experience I can truly say that I have never yet come across a case of primary congenital mental defect. Hardly ever have I seen a case of 'ordinary' uncomplicated, inexplicable retardation, and if I have failed to arrive at a diagnosis, it has been due solely to my own limitations.

By this I do not wish to deny the existence of a small number of children whose brains have, for certain reasons, failed to unfold or whose mental powers cannot develop on account of congenital or acquired hydrocephalus; these are not imbeciles and idiots, but children suffering from microcephalus or hydrocephalus.

For a long time we classified certain children as imbeciles

until it was discovered one day that they were suffering from a disturbance of their protein metabolism, probably congenital, now known as phenylketonuria. The onset of this metabolic disorder is thought to occur right after birth, and it is responsible for a special type of mental handicap. The resulting symptomatology found in children with phenylketonuria is almost identical with post-encephalitic derangements of different etiology.

It is not very long ago that severe autism in childhood was labelled idiocy, until Kanner and many others who followed him taught us to devote special attention to this group of children.

Furthermore, the last twenty years' experience with cerebral palsied children has shown that a small proportion of these children are well developed intellectually and thus able to receive proper schooling. We have learned to pay particular attention to the functioning of the sensory organs of these children. Of one particular group, namely, the athetotics, 60 to 70 per cent are either hard of hearing or suffer to some degree from high-tone deafness.

As one more example, we might consider the problem of crossed dominance or mixed laterality, on the diagnosis of which increasingly more attention is gradually being focused. It is important to realize that there are not only left-handed persons (about 4 per cent of the total population), but also according to recent investigations there are only about 49 per cent fully right-handed persons and the rest, about 47 per cent, are of crossed laterality.[1] Thus a large section amounting to almost half the population are subject to some degree of laterality disturbances. Closely associated with these are disorders of speech leading to stammering, also difficulties with reading and writing, including various types of alexia and agraphia and furthermore, disturbances of co-ordination of voluntary movement that may lead to loss of orientation and thus may give rise to psychotic and neurotic features. One inquiry revealed that in a school attended by several hundred children, all those pupils showing behavioural difficulties as well as slowness in learning were of mixed laterality.

These examples should serve to underline the importance of making every endeavour to come to a rational diagnosis so as to enable us to employ the appropriate therapeutic measures.

2. Treatment

Here I wish to express my conviction that every retarded child, no matter how backward, requires some form of treatment, and I have even come to the conclusion that we have failed these children whenever an active therapy has been omitted. There are quite a large number of therapeutic possibilities, medical and physical as well as educational. In ordinary school education the children are taught as a group while in curative education each single child has to be assessed and handled according to his particular disorder, and therein lies the principal difference between the two.

I should like to give as an example the treatment of Down's syndrome children.

The medical treatment of choice is the therapy which Haubold described some years ago.[2] Details of this are to be found in his own publications, and all Down's syndrome children can derive benefit from it. Yet I do not think that by this treatment the condition itself can be fundamentally altered. The children remain affected by Down's syndrome but are given the chance of a healthier life and a longer maturing process, that is, a longer developmental phase, than without this therapy. The onset of senile changes that otherwise often commence with puberty can be delayed for many years. Hence a Down's syndrome child is enabled to continue to learn if given the facilities.

There is also an educational therapy which has been arrived at from a peculiarity shown by Down's syndrome children who start school. Not only do they become restless for lack of power of concentration, but they are incapable of drawing a straight line. Whenever they draw, circular and curved lines are produced. If one tries to fit this into the whole picture of Down's syndrome it will be found that the feeble motor-functions of these children prevent them from forming the concept of a straight line. The power of uprightness is under-developed; hence the head is bowed, the back arched, the fingers plump and flabby, owing to a laxity of the joints. Their gait is knock-kneed and here, too, the straightness is missing. Thus, one of the first tasks will be to teach them to draw straight lines and this can be achieved after some time by many Down's syndrome children.[3] Only when this has been accomplished can one introduce the writing of single letters. It will take several years before the Down's syndrome child attains an understanding for the written and printed word — but it can be done! By this the child will have been led, part of the way at least, into human civilized life. It is wrong to think that these children are ineducable. Many of them are educable even though to a limited extent only. And to attain even this limited amount of education is perhaps the most significant and deciding factor for the child's personality.

The curative approach to the autistic child has to come from quite a different direction. When observing these children one is struck by the fundamental disturbance of contact, which is not only confined to the psychological level, but reaches deeply into their physiological and metabolic processes. Significantly, we find that in most cases such autism is only towards human beings. Towards animals, plants and inanimate objects, the behaviour can be quite the opposite of withdrawal. The child and the object become so closely integrated that the child can hardly free himself and a 'fixation' to an object thus ensues. This fixation can suddenly be released again, only to attach itself to some other object or person. In this way the child becomes deprived of a full relationship with the whole world of other objects. He becomes one-tracked, narrowed, as if walking on a tightrope.

Associated with this is another conspicuous symptom — the appalling poverty of affections. Neither love and hate nor sympathy and antipathy are experienced. Such a child can become a fixed automaton. Curative education can achieve astonishing results if an effort is made to understand the child's behaviour from the aspect of these cardinal symptoms. The process of freeing the child from the one-sided fixation must be the aim and group therapy in particular is an essential means to that end. Observation of these children will reveal a reduced amount of motor activity and a shallow respiration. If we start to enliven their motility, to arouse and harmonize their movements with musical rhythms, with singing and rhythmical exercises, then much can be achieved. It is very impressive to see such children forget their fixations for minutes and even hours and assume quite a normal behaviour when engaged in common games or in folk dancing. Here again we are not dealing with ineducable imbeciles but with sick children in need of special care.

The curative education of spastic children is primarily concerned with physiotherapy of the paralysed muscular system and this is its starting point. Daily active and passive exercises regularly carried out are the basic element of re-education. If exercises are started early enough only a very small percentage of spastic children will eventually be unable to stand and to walk and to move freely to some extent. The longer we postpone active treatment and the more we are content with reassuring the parents, the less help will be given to these children. We should not forget, however, that children with cerebral palsy are among the most severely handicapped pupils in the field of curative education. In them it becomes apparent that there is not only the incapacity of the limbs and of the whole locomotor system, but also that the perceptual function is almost invariably affected. This in turn causes difficulties in the forming of concepts, and it is at this point that curative education sets in. Spastic and athetotic children of school age should be taught to form concepts by learning to grasp and understand the perceptual world around them. A training in attentiveness, awareness and in the use of their powers of observation is the first step. For example, it is not because of their motor disturbance that such children are unable to draw a house, but because the motor disorder has shattered their world of gestalt and form and therefore they simply do not know what a house really looks like. To them doors, windows, chimneys and walls are separate entities which they cannot fit together into a whole. We are mistaken at the outset if we believe that we can help them just by inventing all sorts of devices by means of which they are enabled to write. Their distortion is at the centre and curative education must approach them from that aspect.

In a similar way it is not to the point to open up the world of sound to a deaf child only by means of hearing aids. These children need the hearing aids, but still more important are their deeply rooted psychological disturbances. These disorders lie in the emotional sphere and require skilled curative care. The emotions and feelings of the deaf child are as primitive and undeveloped as the motor functions of the spastic child. The child is noisy and aggressive and the reason is not the deafness as such, but the lack of cultivation of his feelings. The deaf child lacks the ability to listen and to be aware of the needs and requirements of other people. He must be trained for this in order to counteract this debility and handicap.

3. Education

A few more words about *education*. Again I must put forward the basic assumption that only a very small minority of retarded children are completely unable to go to school and to participate in lessons. Most of the others, irrespective of their higher or lower IQ, require regular teaching. They are even able up to a point to follow the lessons corresponding to their chronological age if given by a suitable teacher. In our schools in Scotland we have some 250 children in need of special care and for the last nine years we have undertaken the experiment of grouping them in school according to age but irrespective of their handicaps. Thus Down's syndrome, post-encephalitic, autistic, neurotic and maladjusted children of the same age all sit together and take part in the same lessons. The method of teaching in our school is based on the principles developed by Rudolf Steiner (Waldorf education) which gives a greater measure of liberty to the teacher. It is an amazing fact that all the children and young people are able to follow these lessons to some degree. This teaching takes place every morning for about two hours and then the classes of twenty to thirty children are divided up into smaller groups and receive special lessons in accordance with their abilities and disabilities. Many of them have been able to learn reading and writing in this way and what is more important, they have taken in what other children of their age are also able to take in. This makes them part of civilized humankind; they are no longer segregated and made into outcasts. The many perversions that we find today in the maladjusted and retarded child are partly due to our modern civilization, which has brought them in its wake. As we have inflicted these wounds it is up to us to do everything in our power to tend them, even if they cannot be healed all at once. Every child has a right to be educated and there is no justification to speak of ineducable children, apart from a small minority, as has been said, not amounting to more than 1 or 2 per cent of all backward and handicapped children.

Our deaf, blind and spastic children do not at present attend the regular classes. They are taught in special classes and only some years later will they be ready to join the regular school.

4. Care

Lastly I wish to say something about the fourth section — that of *care*. In my opinion, the more our understanding of the true nature of the 'special care' child grows, the fewer institutions and residential special schools will be needed for such children. I regard these arrangements as an unavoidable transitional stage, necessary until we physicians as well as the teachers and especially the parents once more realize that the family is the proper place for each of these children. It is there and nowhere else that they, like all children, are 'at home.' This is their natural nest, the place where they feel sheltered and secure. We fully realize that today this ideal can be fulfilled only to a very small extent because both the social conditions and the enlightenment of parents lag far behind. Nevertheless, we must gradually try to bring it about that in all large and small cities the maladjusted and retarded child will have the possibility to go to school together with other children. There will certainly always be special types of children who require care and education in residential schools or institutions. Severe post-encephalitic disturbances, infantile schizophrenia and autistic conditions need a change of environment that can provide treatment and education at the same time. A spastic child that is wanted by the parents definitely belongs in the family and should receive education and treatment in adequately equipped day centres. Ninety-five per cent of all Down's syndrome children belong in their families and ought to take part in the same lessons as other children. Whenever possible the parents should be reminded that it is their own children who are at stake and that these children's education, development and care are ultimately their responsibility. I am aware that at present this cannot always be achieved, yet it should be aimed for. In my opinion it would be a serious error in judgment to advise wealthy and adaptable parents to deprive a Down's syndrome or a spastic or a post-encephalitic child of his family in order to avoid his disturbing influence. No such mistake should ever be made. This may be a grave statement, but I am convinced that we have to acquire a new moral outlook regarding these matters.

The curative care of retarded children, apart from the obvious and undisputed requirement of accommodating them in excellent hygienic buildings with adequate air, light and space, is one of the most difficult tasks of child psychiatry. The one thing these children need most of all is surroundings where they feel at home, where they know that they are accepted and treated as equals. The real need of these children cannot be fulfilled by employed personnel and nursing staff, and by teachers appearing daily. They must be placed into family groups and this is what we try to do in our schools in Scotland. Their 'mothers' and 'fathers' live with them all the time; they have their meals together and play and work together as is natural in a family. It is a matter of all or nothing, just as we know it from the physiology of the cardiac muscle. It is a decision that in time will have to be faced. Only when this social law concerning the care of children has been observed will we be able to achieve true therapeutic success. Much more should be said about this point, but here it could only be touched upon.

If the four spheres described are woven together into a true pattern, there will appear what I regard as the ideal image of a future practice of child psychiatry. It will not be a matter of psychology or any other isolated branch of science, but simply a knitting together of many disciplines, creatively joining in a common effort. Neurologists, psychiatrists, teachers, physiotherapists, craftsmen, gardeners, sociologists — they will all have to co-operate if true help is to reach the handicapped child.

5

Basic Issues of Curative-Educational Diagnosis and Therapy

1. What is curative education?

Since Rudolf Steiner held the Curative Education Course in summer 1924, curative education, which had been inaugurated by him, has not only grown considerably but all curative-educational aspirations and efforts seem to have received an immediate fresh impetus. The publication of Homburger's book on the psychopathology of childhood in 1925, regular curative education congresses in Germany and America, the Child Guidance movement which developed in the western countries during the 1920s, the gradual development of the education of paralysed children in America and the intense awakening to the psychiatry of childhood are the main indications of this outset.

Today the care and education of children with behavioural problems has evolved into a social issue which has become a priority of debate and work in all civilized countries. As a result, however, serious questions have arisen for which there is hardly a solution yet. These questions are grouped around one main question which can be simply put in the words, 'What is curative education?' That is to say, 'What is the position of curative education within the system of the sciences and within the human course of action as such?' Apart from those existing at the University of Zurich and recently at the University of Erlangen, there is no chair in curative education and the question of whether curative education should be specified as a field of medicine or a domain of education is still open.

In 1941 Heinrich Hanselmann, professor for curative education in Zurich, wrote a book reflecting on this question. He reviewed the literature on this subject and tried to define his own approach:

> So we give the following definition: Special education (curative education) is the theory of the scientifically guided understanding of the causes and effects of the physical-emotional-mental condition and behaviour of developmentally inhibited children and young people and their instruction, education and care.[1]

Of course this sentence is not a definition but simply a phrasing of what is known anyway. It does not state anything more than what has been done since the beginnings of curative education.

Professor Asperger says in the introduction of his recently published book, *Heilpädagogik:*

> We will call curative education the science which, based on a biological knowledge of abnormal child personalities, aims to find mainly educational ways to treat cognitive and sensory deficiencies, and mental and emotional disorders during childhood and youth. The best human guidance resulting from an understanding of the human being can, so we think, influence disturbed personalities in a positive way.

From this, too, nothing much can be gleaned apart from what is known already, however, a phrase stands out which is not part of Hanselmann's wording. 'The best human guidance resulting from an understanding of the human being' is a significant consideration and needs to be taken seriously especially since Asperger points out subsequently that five different 'wellsprings' contribute to curative education. As such he mentions: psychiatry, pediatrics, psychology, social science and education. Therefore these five subjects appear to be individual disciplines, separate from curative education, which contribute support and substance but are not curative education themselves.

But curative education is by no means just a mixture of these five wellsprings. Instead for the last few years it has striven to gain an understanding of itself as a coherent discipline. And again there is the question, 'What is curative education?'

What the above-mentioned definitions have in common is that they refer to the treatment of children with learning difficulties. Asperger describes 'mainly educational ways to treat' and 'guidance,' and Hanselmann mentions 'instruction, education and care.' This needs to be taken into account because it acknowledges that the practice of curative education is at least as important as the understanding of it. However, if this practice is supposed to be based on scientific methods then it needs to be preceded by understanding because only a practice which is guided by understanding can be regarded as scientific. Yet curative-educational practice can only originate in curative-educational understanding and this is nothing else but true diagnosis. Only if there is a development of curative-educational diagnosis will we be able to speak of a curative-educational practice generated by such an understanding. In this way the quite general question, 'What is curative education?' becomes a more specific one, 'What is curative-educational diagnosis?'

It is (according to the definitions above) the understanding 'of the physical-emotional-mental condition and behaviour of developmentally inhibited children and young people' or 'of cognitive and sensory deficiencies, and mental and emotional disorders during childhood and youth.'

I think it is a valid thing to say that at the moment we still suffer a complete lack of curative-educational diagnosis; because the developmental inhibitions, cognitive deficiencies, mental and emotional disorders are still being assessed according to the wellsprings of curative education. What I mean is this: if a child diagnosed with learning difficulties in such a way that, for instance, an insufficient development of a certain part of the brain is identified as the cause of his developmental inhibition, then this is a medical and not a curative-educational diagnosis. If you establish a certain level of IQ for the same child then this also is not a curative-educational diagnosis but a psychological one. Of course both diagnoses are helpful and should be considered at any rate but they are not curative-educational diagnoses. If another child who shows aggressive behaviour is diagnosed in a way that his behaviour is seen as the result of the failings of his mother during his early childhood, then this assessment is a psychiatric but not a curative-educational diagnosis.

That is why it is time that curative educators developed an awareness of the fact that psychological, psychiatric and medical diagnoses, and assessment of the social environment and of the educational achievements of the child — thus everything which stems from the wellsprings described by Asperger — are nothing but diagnostic aids which are needed as long as there is no true curative-educational diagnosis.

A curative educator cannot dispense with psychology and psychiatry but he is not a real curative educator as long as he has not found his specific ground to stand on and as long as he interprets the child in his treatment only from the viewpoint of neurology, psychiatry or psychology.

And there is another point. It is still common practice to classify children with developmental deficiencies according to their level of intelligence and as a result they are classified as being debile, imbecile or as idiots. But this classification is usually misused in a such way that it is turned into a diagnosis right away and a child is identified as being debile or imbecile without the doctor or psychologist even bothering to underpin such classifications with appropriate diagnosis. This is the result of a disastrous overestimation of intellect which insists on using the level of intelligence as a criterion for human existence. Consequently fully adequate children and young people are often condemned to a life behind walls. Basically there is no such condition as 'debility.' At least I have never encountered it in twenty-five years of curative-educational practice. This idea of 'debility' is a hypothetical absurdity which could only be misused to such an extent because there was as yet no curative-educational diagnosis.

Of course psychology, neurology and psychiatry and their various methods of diagnosis are being introduced to curative education; but it is time that curative education developed its own diagnostic values on the basis of a true understanding of itself. And the question is going to be raised as to what curative-educational diagnosis can really be, in contrast to all the other diagnoses mentioned here.

2. Curative-educational diagnosis and therapy

In the curative-educational course mentioned at the start of these explanations, Rudolf Steiner not only gave essential explanations of certain aberrations of child behaviour but in the practical part of the course he also described real children, and by means of these descriptions he demonstrated how one can establish a curative-educational diagnosis. For example, he describes in detail the form of the skull, the shape of certain parts of the face, the connection between the development of the limbs and the form of the head and he uses all these detailed facts, by putting them in context, to define a nearly perfect idea of the child's being. Thus something quite essential has taken place which so far has hardly been introduced to general curative education.

For example when Rudolf Steiner says: 'Observe now how the head is narrow *here* (in front) on both sides, and pressed back; so we have in this boy the symptom of narrow-headedness, a sign that the intellectual system is but little permeated with will.'[2] Or when he refers to the same child's open mouth and then explains that from this you can see 'that in this child the lower man is not fully under the control and mastery of the upper man,'[3] then these statements represent the first indications of curative-educational diagnosis. This is because the observation of the body organization itself reveals the ways of the spirit and soul.

This is not a trivial form of physiognomy but a thorough consideration of the human shape from which the main emotional patterns can be deducted. Since Ernst Kretschmer's studies proved that there is a connection between the body and character these methods should no longer be presented with the same barriers. Because there is scientific evidence that an asthenic disposition is associated with a schizoid temperament and a pyknic disposition with a cycloid temperament. But Kretschmer's classifications are mere contours; large but unelaborated sketches which still need to be thoroughly worked on in detail.

But this will only be possible if the *threefold structure* of the body and soul is taken as the archetype of an understanding of the human being.[4] Then, for example, it will be immediately evident that the asthenic disposition means a preponderance of the upper organization, of the senses and the nerves, and that the pyknic disposition correlates with a preponderance of the lower metabolism-limb organization. And what Kretschmer describes as the athletic disposition is caused by a preponderance of the central, rhythmic organization. As a result, however, these three dispositional types and their associated characteristics are no random phenomena which come about by chance but they are three variants which originate from the human organization in its entirety. They are three versions of a consistent theme.

This, however, leads to another important conclusion. If these types of disposition represent individual realizations of the same theme it is erroneous to think that, for example, one person is solely asthenic and another solely pyknic. Instead it will be accurate to develop the idea that all three typical dispositions exist at the same time in every human being but are balanced and take their effects to different degrees. Only if every person is seen as a harmonious combination of the pyknic, athletic and asthenic disposition, yet at the same time representing an individual balance of these three dispositions, can a true understanding of this phenomenon be developed.

However, it would surely be wrong to use the dispositional types described by Kretschmer as a basis for curative-educational diagnostics. Recent studies have shown that it is extremely difficult to find evidence of these types in children during childhood development, and the researcher Wilfried Zeller who is known for his thoroughness wrote: 'Furthermore, it must be said, that during the development due to the superimposition of developmental conditions, the Kretschmer's types can only be differentiated with great difficulty, if at all.'

On the other hand, whoever has encountered a substantial number of children with behaviour problems cannot fail to find certain common characteristics which gradually make him think of some grouping or category. But in doing this he will only get somewhere if he avoids arbitrarily singling out certain types and tampering with some superficial kind of physiognomy. In the same way as Kretschmer, unknowingly, traced the threefold concept of the human being and consequently was able to identify disposition and character from the powers of creation themselves, in this way the formative forces in the development of the child need to be traced which, if they work disharmoniously, create forms which can be seen and described.

Surely this is the great learning experience for curative educators; that they can find formative and developmental tendencies in abnormal children, which in more or less normal children remain hidden because there these formative tendencies are balanced. In the children encountered in curative education, so-called abnormalities become evident of which otherwise we can only form a vague idea; here is revealed what otherwise remains a secret. And the object of curative-educational diagnostics (which is based on reality) is to trace these formative tendencies and identify them in the individual child; because abnormality and aberration are nothing new, nothing that does not exist otherwise. Abnormality is rather something becoming visible which exists otherwise but because it is kept in a balance, is not immediately evident.

The development of these formative tendencies which exist in everyone and which, if developed in an unbalanced way, result in the conditions we see in children in need of soul care, will form the foundations of a future curative-educational diagnostics and the therapy following from it.

The doctor, too, will have to learn about these formative and developmental tendencies but he will integrate them into his knowledge of remedies. The educator again will use this knowledge of the human being by taking it as a guideline for curriculum development and for forming the personal relationship between teacher and student.

Curative education is not about remedies; in most cases these will be indispensable but they are the doctor's concern. Curative education is not about teaching either. This will be necessary as well, it will even be a vital element of what needs to be done for a child in need of soul care; but these classes will have to be held within the realm of education and must not be confused with curative education.

It is therapeutic intervention which lies within the field of curative education, not the remedy nor the instruction. If necessary learning experiences can be modified by curative-educational interventions: lower or higher pace, simplified or more complex, concrete or more abstract. As with everything alive the limits are not set in stone. Yet curative-educational intervention is not education but curative education.

This will always involve interventions supposed to restore the disturbed balance of the formative and developmental tendencies of the developing child. This can happen in many ways.

Music and singing, eurythmy and curative eurythmy, speech and gestures, drawing and painting, craft and memory training can be applied.

The right course of action, however, will only be brought about if the insight into human nature results in guidance as a carefully directed, creative process. The concept of the human being characterized by its threefoldness as it was developed by Rudolf Steiner is the archetype of all curative-educational diagnostics. This threefoldness bears the most varied developmental tendencies and the following can give some examples to make evident what is supposed to be an emerging curative-educational diagnostics and therapy based on scientific methods.

By this no claims are made to be complete; it is only a first approach which, however, originates from decades of experience. Individual developmental tendencies will be described which reflect what otherwise remains hidden within the human being.

3. Hydrocephaly and microcephaly

Teachers should learn, so they were advised by Rudolf Steiner, to distinguish between children with large heads and those with small heads even when they look at a normally developed child. During the teachers' conference at the Waldorf School in Stuttgart on February 6, 1923 he points out this difference and emphasizes how important it is for teachers to gain a clear picture of this. He then describes the child with a *large head:*

> If you notice that a child has a slight tendency to not pay attention, to not take in properly what the teacher is developing in the class, one could also say he is too much of a sanguine or a phlegmatic, then you have to try in some way or another to stimulate the formative forces, to enable the child to be more attentive to his surroundings.

About children with a *smaller head* he says that they tend to 'be just self-occupied in soul and spirit and thus also in body' and as a result will develop into children with a tendency of brooding. Just as the child with a large head, due to his fleetingness, 'has too little inclination to have a discerning imagination, throws everything together in imagination, and cannot properly discern,' so the child with the small head is only insufficiently capable of conceptual synthesis and has greatest difficulty to envision things; as a result the child with a small head becomes 'a philistine in art.' What we see here only as a disposition, only as tendencies, can gradually increase, become one-sided and in its extreme lead to what is represented in the hydrocephalic child on one hand and in the microcephalic child on the other.

Although the pathological-physiological background of hydrocephaly can be quite different from that of microcephaly, both conditions are still basic curative-educational patterns which need to be regarded as an entity. For this reason I will prioritise curative-educational rather than medical aspects.

The *hydrocephalic* child suffers from the extreme size of his head. It usually happens in that some time after birth, approximately during the third or fourth month, the child's skull begins to grow and gradually becomes overpoweringly large. At the same time the fontanelle remains open so that there is an incomplete ossification of the skull. The child learns to sit very late and often has no chance to learn to stand upright or walk. This can also be accompanied by spastic paralysis of the limbs.

On the other hand it can be noticed that these children begin to speak at a remarkably young age and are often able to express themselves in well formed sentences even at the beginning of their second year of life. They show extraordinary language skills and their conversation is often very advanced for their age.

If these children learn to walk later they tread the ground only with their toes and remain unconfident in their movements. It often happens that these children eventually lose their vision and gradually go blind.

If you try to gain a deeper understanding of such a person you will find that these children make little contact with their environment; usually they are surprisingly friendly, content and likable. They have traits which used to be called affable; they have a kind of aristocratic gentleness which is associated with an unearthliness which makes them almost adorable. The size of their head which often resembles a dome gives them an air which can make others feel in awe.

With *microcephalic* children it is different. During infancy the head lags behind in growth; the fontanelle begins to close during the first months of life and the ossification of the skull is soon complete. If there are no other issues than microcephaly these children soon learn to walk and they are restless and very mobile. They try to touch, to smell, to feel, to master everything. Language skills, however, are much delayed and it is often not before the age of four or five that they learn individual words.

Observing these children more closely you find that they are intensely involved with the earthly world. What the child with a small head is lacking — the 'conceptual synthesis,' the ability to 'envision' things — is more pronounced in the microcephalic child. Imagination is almost non-existent. The world represented by the basic senses (sight, taste, smell) is an immediate reality and every attempt to form ideas tends to fail miserably. In an extreme case such a child will skip from sensation to sensation and will hold on to them using his limbs but not his thoughts.

During further development, as these children grow up, their limbs develop into massive grasping organs. The hands become big and strong, the legs weighty and long; the lower jaw grows bigger but the skull and its small receding forehead remains static and rigid. Often these children are reluctant, moody, self-centred. Wherever they are, everything in their surrounds becomes untidy. They always get dirty because they feel almost insatiably attracted to everything material.

What is organized and harmonious in the hydrocephalic child appears here in disarray and destructive. Yet both tendencies exist in every child and every person but are more or less kept in balance. But if this balance is disturbed, and the tendency associated with a large head in the hydrocephalus or the tendency associated with a small head in the microcephalus become too dominant, the consequences will be the conditions described.

If we probe into the causes of these tendencies we see that hydrocephalus in children represents a disposition which tends to hold on to the embryonic stage of development for too long; the head remains as the overemphasized organization is retained to the extreme. In microcephalic children, however, the drive towards death, rigidification, and incarnation is too strong and dominant.

In his first lecture of the cycle called *Anthroposophy* on January 19, 1924 Rudolf Steiner described the relationship of the human being to the environment in so far as the human being encounters this environment through the head on one side and through the limbs on the other. He commented on the head organization with the following words: 'There is a human soul but nature can only get to it by becoming an illusion.'

This is a characterization of the hydrocephalic child's relationship to the world. Nature itself has become a merely illusory phenomenon. It is captured in abstract language but the access to reality is missing. But this access to reality can only develop if the limbs are intensely activated. This is the therapeutic task of the curative educator encountering hydrocephaly either as a disposition or as a fully developed condition. For this reason Rudolf Steiner said about the treatment of a hydrocephalic child for whom he had to care when he was a young man: 'The secret of the matter lay in the care and attention given to the movement of the limbs; through this, it came about that the hydrocephalic condition disappeared.'[5]

In the human soul the limb organization and the experience of the world are related in a way which Rudolf Steiner described in the following words: 'There is a nature, but the human being can only get to it inasmuch as he lets it destroy him.'

This, however, is the accurate description of how the microcephalic child behaves towards the environment. The natural powers invade these children too deeply and too directly. The ability to keep things at a distance and to turn them into ideas is not strong enough; as a result the human being is overpowered by the world and cannot sustain himself as an independent personality.

However, the day consciousness of every human being develops through the harmonious orchestration of hydrocephalic and microcephalic tendencies. Being 'not-quite-awake-yet' in the mornings is typical for the child with a large head; therefore he has difficulties perceiving differences, and Rudolf Steiner advised to cool such a child's head in the mornings. In the hydrocephalic child this has been taken a step further; he does not pass through the morning gateway of birth into the day but remains behind it as if concealed by a veil.

The child with a small head already slips into a state of light sleep while he is still awake. He broods, the natural powers are already approaching it, and Rudolf Steiner advised 'to suggest to parents that, two or three times a week they give their child a stomach poultice that stays on in the night.' In the microcephalic child this has developed a step further. He walks this world lightly asleep.

Guided by this information, however, the curative educator will be able to find his mode of therapy. The hydrocephalic child needs to be led from morning doziness into day consciousness by active movement of his limbs. The microcephalic child can be raised from the night sleepiness to the day by activating his thoughts.

But it needs to be noted that *every* child tends to one of either condition and each child's disposition should be identified in order to provide appropriate help.

4. Speech and its components

As wakeful day consciousness results from the harmonious balance of the hydrocephalic and the microcephalic tendency and thus prepares the foundations for the existence of the soul within the body, in the same way an activity of the soul evolves within the day consciousness which is of utmost importance for the curative educator. This activity of the soul is *speech*; and it is fairly safe to say that there is hardly any child in need of soul care who does not suffer from some form of speech disorder. Basically you could even say: speech disorders are an indicator of the child's need for soul care. This can vary from the mildest speech rhythm disorders to a complete inability to form words, from the most severe text blindness to stuttering and stammering.

Curative educators who learn to listen attentively to the language skills of their children will be able to master another field of curative-educational diagnostics. But speech disorders belong to a different sphere than the one which brings about the day consciousness. We shall explore this sphere now.

Every child with a speech disorder displays symptoms which are closely associated with this disorder. The stutterer, for instance, also shows a stutter of his handwriting if he has learned to write, and at times he also 'stutters' when walking or breathing, and all his motor skills will be affected by the stutter to some degree. A child, for example, who does not learn any language skills due to deafness will show severe motor abnormalities; will either move in an aggressive and exaggerated way or will be droopy and listless. On the other hand, a child with marked symptoms of palsy will also show marked speech problems; in fact, there is no real palsy of the motor system without speech being affected as well.

These are observations which belong to the daily experience of the curative educator. From this it can immediately be seen that on one hand speech is fully integrated in the element of movement and in the system of motor functions. On the other hand there is another element; the simple observation that deaf or hearing-impaired children cannot acquire speech shows that hearing as a whole is at least as closely associated with speech as movement. But it would be far too simple and easy to conclude that a deaf child cannot speak just because he does not hear spoken words. There are a lot of children who remain mute or become mute although they should be able to hear excellently since their acoustic organs are in perfect working order. Though there are children whose middle and internal ear is severely damaged in parts and who, through continuous exercise, can still be taught accurate hearing.

Whoever has experience in this field over many years will gradually begin to understand why Rudolf Steiner in some parts of his lectures spoke about movement and hearing as counterparts, for example, 'A large part of musical experience consists of holding oneself back, holding back movement.'[6] Such statements and observations show that hearing can only take place if movement has come to a harmonious rest. Listening requires a 'quiet space.' But motor activity permanently invades this space and a person with overly active movement will have little capacity for listening; the one who listens attentively, however, will be a person of deliberate movement.

And where motor activity, which flows upwards from the limbs, joins what flows downwards from the head as listening, the basic elements of speech are formed. The listening element which bears words and sound and the motor element which can bring these words to verbalization are the two basic elements of speech. Dominance of motor activity, dominance of listening or a disharmonious flowing together of both will cause essential speech disorders.

But if this concept of listening-speaking-moving, which has been described here, is acknowledged as another element of curative-educational diagnostics the individual disposition of each child will become obvious. Then it will be observed that in a boy with partial palsy of his arms and complete palsy of his legs, speech does not develop because he hardly has any movement. He is not motivated to speak because listening is far too dominant. In another child overly active movement has grown to the extent that it is almost impossible for the limbs to come to a rest. And here again speech does not exist; but it is missing because listening could not develop, as movement constantly interrupts the generation of 'quiet space.' A third child is mute because his legs and arms have become so droopy and are so deeply attached to the element of gravity that from this slow and clumsy co-ordination the lightness of motor speech control could not evolve; although he can hear and understand and at times even listen, speech does not detach itself because movement has fallen too deeply into the realm of gravity.

If you then try to take this a bit further and understand the soul characteristics of these disorders, you will find that all initiative which we carry within ourselves as a fundamental power of the soul is nothing but an element of the motor system which in turn is controlled by the will. The element of laxity, however, and inner languidness — which in psychology is usually described as avolition — is associated with the ability to listen. If listening becomes a predominant attitude, laxity will be the result; if motor activity is too strong, initiative will become overly hastened and rushed.

All this again is expressed in the manner of speaking. Whether children speak so fast that the words are all jumbled together or whether they drag their words to the extent that it seems as if you can see through the gaps between the pickets of a fence, is not just an expression of temperament but of the co-ordinated balance of listening and movement.

But with this the curative educator is provided with a second element for his therapy. Using harmonious rhythmic movement accompanied by music and singing he can try to restore harmonious motor activity in such a way that listening evolves upwards. In the passive child he can try to stir the overly developed listening by activating the will in the limbs through speech and songs of accentuated sounds and tones; in many cases it will take a big drum or even a trumpet to bring about an initial stimulation.

In addition speech disorders should never be directly tackled from language, instead they should be approached from the angle of listening or movement. A wealth of manifold curative-educational interventions will unfold if there is an understanding of this profound context: The limb being exists within movement and there develops the ability of initiative action; this flows upwards and transforms in the larynx into speech motor control.

The head being, insofar as he can hear, exists within listening and there bears the element of laxity. During passive listening, however, tone and words are heard and flow downwards to join the speech motor control in the larynx.

The combination of these two elements bring about a third one, and that is speech.

The harmonious combination of active movement with passive listening create within the child what externally expresses itself as speech.

5. Down's syndrome and cretinism

We encounter a quite different area of human formative tendencies when we see a phenomenon as extraordinary as Down's syndrome children. At first the idea of understanding such a special group by following the principle of a general human formative force may seem far-fetched; but because Down's syndrome children do exist — and for the past fifty years in such big numbers too — there is reason to assume that there is a disposition somewhere in every human being which, even if not usually so apparent, bears in its origin everything which unfolds and fully develops in the Down's syndrome child.

Therefore it is fair to ask what it is exactly that is hidden in ourselves and reveals itself within the spectrum of Down's syndrome. The more you study the various characteristics of a markedly Down's syndrome child, the more individual traits you see which you consistently find in children who are not Down's syndrome as such. An increasing number of these *formes frustes,* as they are called, are being described. There is the flexed little finger on one or both hands; the third eyelid; the angular lid gap; the dry, scaled-off skin; the strangely undeveloped, clumsy hand with the seemingly primitive fingers; the hoarse voice lacking in tone, and more which as a whole form the unmistakable character of Down's syndrome children.

Certain emotional traits are also present in many children who yet do not belong to the group of Down's syndrome. There is a spontaneity which unreservedly turns to every human being; which expects to find and welcome the father in every man and the mother in every woman; a certain cheek combined with a natural sense of shame which often makes these children so charming. From the same bashfulness stems a frequent stubbornness which is difficult to overcome. In some children there is also an intense musicality which seems to be linked to a complete inability to think mathematically. Many of these typical Down's syndrome traits can be individually present in many other children.

If you examine the distribution of Down's syndrome children in Europe and America you soon notice that most of them are born near the coast. An increased frequency can be found in countries like Denmark, Britain and Holland. I also assume that it is safe to conclude from various reports and my own studies that there are a lot more Down's syndrome children in low lands than in the mountains. They seem to like the open spaces, the water, the open sky and the distant horizon.

If you ask now what is the one characteristic of Down's syndrome children, apart from these individual traits, that includes all other traits then you will surely notice that above all many

Down's syndrome children — nearly all of them — represent the same type. Therefore you can often state already at the first glance, 'This is a Down's syndrome child.' This is in contrast to children with hydrocephalus who have each developed their own individuality despite the hydrocephalic tendency, and also in contrast to all other disorders which always allow for the individuality of the personality to shine through. But with Down's syndrome the personality often, indeed mostly, disappears behind the species. And this seems to be the profound fundamental tendency of Down's syndrome: that with Down's syndrome individuality retreats behind the human species. Here the 'human species' becomes evident and openly visible, showing what all human beings have in common, the 'universal nature' on which humankind as a whole is based.

This is the reason why it is frequently and, in my opinion, justifiably pointed out that Down's syndrome children are not fully developed but have remained at embryonic stage. They could be described as grown-up embryos. For this reason they hardly show any characteristics relating to family or nation. I have seen Arab, Indian, Jewish and Slavic Down's syndrome children; Down's syndrome children with English, German, Scandinavian and French parents; none of them was of a certain nationality. First and foremost they were Down's syndrome children who immediately recognized each other as brothers and sisters, welcomed each other as such and were in accordance whenever they met.

This may be correlated to the fact that Down's syndrome children, when they grow up, do not show any concern for sexuality; they remain somewhat sexless in the same way as they remain free of national traits. Therefore they are remarkably free of all the burdens which the individual mortal normally has to shoulder. Carefree and cheerful, open and with a lot of warmth, they seem to be closer to paradise than to sin.

This is also the reason for one outstanding trait of Down's syndrome, the extraordinary ability of facial expression. With a

single gesture they can impersonate another person and this particular ability of impersonation is the same as we find in young
children up to the age of six or seven. The Down's syndrome
child keeps this trait of young children for a long time; he is a
person who after birth has not completely forgotten what had
happened to him before birth. Therefore he is so often, wherever he appears, a gleam of hope in the gloom of the earthly
world and people spontaneously love him. What has not been
individualized in each of us but has remained in a generally par-
adisal state — warmth, openness, a carefree nature, but often
also our inability to assert ourselves as an individual, also our
mocking behaviour, our audacity and laziness — all of what is
universally human, the idea of what St Paul called the first
Adam, all that is the Down's syndrome child within us.

In contrast to this there is another formative tendency which
also expresses itself in people who are similar to each other and
who appear all over the world. Only they are at home especially
where mountains form deep valleys, where sunlight is only
rarely seen and the horizon is obscured. These people are mostly
dark, wizened, half or completely deaf and therefore have only
little speech and can hardly express themselves verbally. They
are often devious, envious and cunning. Their body organization is rigid and often crippled. Despite that there is some
kindness in their eyes at times and whoever has encountered
them closer cannot help liking them. These people suffer from
cretinism.

What presents itself in Down's syndrome as wide and open to
the world is enclosed and rigorous in cretinism. What has been
described as 'universally human' in Down's syndrome has
become an excessive form of personality in cretinism. Children
suffering from cretinism are overly self-centred and selfish.
Hence they are hearing-impaired or deaf because they do not
have the ability of listening attentively. In cretinism individuality
becomes egoistic to the extent that it actually loses its personality
and appears as a uniform regularity. What is envisioned in

gloomy imagination of the common masses — the outlines of this is represented in cretinism.

In contrast to Down's syndrome most people suffering from cretinism have a strong sex drive and have a lot of children who, however, do not always suffer from cretinism.

Cretinism exists in ourselves, as the characteristics described above are present in every human being. The child suffering from cretinism is at the foot of the ladder and the Down's syndrome child stands at the top. The latter has not gained full individualization and therefore remains within the universal while the child of cretinism has exceeded individualization and has thus destroyed it within himself. Between these two extremes all possible nuances can be found which are related to the various stages of individual human development.

For the curative educator, however, these descriptions serve as guidelines for his work. He needs to try to shape the personality of the Down's syndrome child. This will happen through individual instructions which will strengthen memory and encourage conscience. Down's syndrome children are great pagans and teaching them the basics of Christianity is a form of curative-educational therapy. But they also should be present in every group of children in order to enrich them socially and let them contribute what are their immediate qualities: bringing joy and light-heartedness where they have become too scarce.

In cretinism some curative-educational success can be achieved if interventions start early and the hearing impairment can be treated. The sociability that Down's syndrome children naturally possess, needs to be taught to children with cretinism by therapeutic means. They need to be led out of and liberated from their self-rigidity. Love for other people, understanding for the needs of others, is what the cretinism needs. But at the same time this is what continuously overcomes cretinism in ourselves.

6. Summary

With these examples I have tried to demonstrate the way in which curative-educational diagnostics will develop. It will be free of psychological concepts but it will also need to stay free from medical research. It will strive to understand the archetypal formative tendencies of the developing human being and will gradually realize that there are not unlimited possibilities but that there are limited options equivalent to the creative powers of the world.

The hydrocephalic tendency exists in the human being and is constantly balanced by the microcephalic tendency; the hydro-cephalic formative force takes effect in the head organization, the microcephalic formative force in the limbs. But it also takes effect outwith the human being and can be seen in the animal, for instance when polyp and medusa develop. The medusa, the jellyfish, is a direct representation of hydrocephaly whereas the polyp as its counterpart represents the microcephalic tendency.

In the same way, listening and moving work together. All mobility of the limbs and all of motor functions originate from here; in contrast to this, however, there is restfulness, laxity, listening. Whenever molluscs develop in the animal world — snails, shellfish, cuttlefish — they are a representation of this listening tendency. In the same way as the ear is encapsulated inside the skull, as the skull itself is the element of rest in the human being, in the same way the shellfish and the snail are encapsulated inside their shells. And if we hold the shell of a shellfish to our ear silence becomes audible within it. If, however, as in the cuttlefish or even in the octopus, listening is interrupted, moving limbs eerily unfold from the head.

There are similar findings regarding the Down's syndrome tendency and the contrasting cretinoid formative development. But it is always the human being who stands between the 'upper' and the 'lower' tendency, trying to keep both in balance.

Only if he is successful will he achieve his true human existence: speech, day consciousness, individual personality.

The human being is a part of heaven as well as a part of the earth and needs the balancing harmony of both to fulfill his human existence on earth. *This is the great task of curative education, that it opens up the path in every child to being human, to being mediator.* This will be achieved in some cases, in others not. But the attempt always needs to be made. Because if there is no immediate success the mere intention to do something good is as valid. The influence of this intention will continue and at another time, when this child again starts its journey into the earthly world, it will act as the healing medicine.

As a curative educator you need to be aware that often results are not immediately forthcoming but that they take great ages of time until the child's soul has transformed what it had received as a therapeutic intervention. And there is hardly anybody for whom Lessing's words at the end of his work, *The Education of the Human Race,* are more true than for the child in need of soul care, 'And how much then should I miss? Is not a whole Eternity mine?'

Again and again each human soul tries anew to join the eternal formative tendencies of the powers of creation within itself and to bring them into a balance. Whenever this fails curative education as a mediator is entitled to apply healing interventions.

Curative Education, Modern Civilization and Social Community

Die drei Grundlagen der Heilerziehung.

(Ca 3000 Worte)

Am Ende des vorigen Jahrhunderts begann der Zerfall der menschlichen Gesellschaft. Die Ordnungen, die bis dahin ~~die~~ die Haltung des einzelnen Menschen bestimmt hatten, begannen zu zerbrechen. Die Familie, "Dorfgemeinschaft", "Zunft", der Staat selbst, ob klein oder groß, verlor ~~seine~~ realen Kräfte; damit ihre Bedeutung. Zunächst merkten das die Menschen nicht sehr; erst allmählich, je weiter sich dieser Zerfall bis in die Gegenwart herein ausbreitete, umso ansichtiger ~~wider den Geistern~~ wurde es Einigen.

Historisch geht dieser Umwandlungs- & Zerstörungsprozeß 300 Jahre zurück. Als 1648 der Westfälische Friede geschlossen wurde, war der erste, große Zerrüttungsprozeß der sozialen Ordnung abgeschlossen. Der Dreißigjährige Krieg hatte die Grundmauern der menschlichen Gesellschafts-Ordnung stark erschüttert. Wallenstein, eine der bedeutsamsten Persönlichkeiten dieser Zeit hat das ~~ge~~ verspürt & schon damals versucht, soziale Neubildungen durchzuführen. Er verwaltete seine großen Ländereien in einer, man würde heute sagen, "sozialen" Art & er formte auch als erster Feldherr eine internationale Armee.

Der zweite Stoß im Rahmenwerk der europäischen Sozial-Ordnung war die Französische Revolution. (1789 das Jahr) ~~brachte~~ die Fundamente der Gesellschafts-Ordnung so sehr ins Wanken, daß von da an die Auflösung nicht mehr langsam, sondern schneller & schneller vor sich ging. Die napoleonischen Kriege, die unglückseligen Kittversuche Metternichs, das Jahr 1848, die sozialen Gesetzgebungen ~~Bis~~ Bismarks, die Formation der Marxistischen Arbeiter-Vereine & Parteien lösten den von innen her hohl gewordenen Bau des hierarchischen Bürger- & Adelstums auf & am Ende des vorigen Jahrhunderts war davon nichts ~~mehr übrig geblieben~~

The Three Foundations of Curative Education. Manuscript p.1.
Camphill 1948

6

The Three Foundations
of Curative Education

At the end of the nineteenth century, the decline of human society began. The social order which until then had determined the attitude of the individual began to collapse. The family, the village community, the guilds, the state itself, whether big or small, lost their real powers and therefore their significance. At first this was not much noticed and only gradually, the more this decline reached into present times, the more obvious it became to some people.

Historically this process of transformation and destruction goes back three hundred years. When in 1648 the Treaty of Westphalia was concluded, the first substantial process of eroding the social order was over. The Thirty Years' War had profoundly shaken human society to its very foundations. Wallenstein, one of the most important people of this time, had sensed that and already then had tried to enforce social regeneration. He managed his great estates in a way which today would be called 'social' and he was also the first military leader who formed an international army.

The second blow to the framework of the European social order was the French Revolution. The year 1789 shook the foundations of society to an extent that disintegration no longer happened gradually but at an ever faster pace. The Napoleonic

Wars, Metternich's hapless attempts to patch things up, the year 1848, Bismarck's Social Legislation, the formation of Marxist workers' associations and parties eroded the no longer significant hierarchy of the bourgeoisie and aristocracy from within, and at the end of the last century nothing was left of them but a façade. The devastated Central European cities of today are the true picture of what had already been prepared at the end of the nineteenth century.

To pull down this façade was and will continue to be the deed of the twentieth century. The disasters of two world wars have, to some extent, finished what had been started by the Thirty Years' War and was continued by the French Revolution and the other social revolutions.

Through these enormous traumas, however, every individual person was deeply impacted. The organic structures of the social order which had existed until then dissolved those safeguards that were in place for everyone when they were born and grew up, thereby forcing the individual to rely upon his own resources. During the past two decades the strongest element of human society, the family, has also broken down due to the rise of Bolshevism in the East and the horrendous nationalism in Germany, Italy, Spain, etc. Already before and after the First World War the foundations of marriage were destabilized. Its sacramental fabric had become an empty shell and the rationalism of thought did not replace this sacramental content with an equally powerful core element. Consequently marriages broke down and turned more and more into trial relationships that had lost their emotionally nurturing foundation, becoming merely a way of ensuring progeny.

It was a distressing experience, especially in medical practice, to witness the loss of motherly instincts. Nursing babies, feeding toddlers, educating children were no longer just natural acts but became problems with which mothers and fathers were unable to cope. Women's infertility was more and more on the increase and today every 'civilized' country has to establish baby advice

Karl König in the Camphill Community

centres, marriage and family advice centres, hoping to counter-act the disintegration of families.

Despite this social and societal fiasco children are born, in some countries even more children than 'wished for.' They grow up without guidance or protection, at random, as is the way with modern life.

Does it really come as a surprise that there are more and more children who are no longer capable of being 'normal'? At the beginning of this century two or three out of a hundred children needed special education. This has increased to eleven to twelve in a hundred. This means that twelve out of a hundred, a hundred and twenty out of a thousand, twelve hundred out of ten thousand children cannot be provided with a normal upbringing in a family nor with regular education.

And why should our children act 'normally' if they are put in a society whose core is utterly and completely in ruins? Why should they wish to live as if nothing has happened on earth and things are fine anyway according to the picture painted by the newspapers and narrow-minded politicians? This world in which children and adults have become a commodity on the employment market and a digit in the unitary state? A world in which from birth onwards everything has been set so that the developing person will find every advantage and condition imaginable apart from one: to be a human being!

More and more children grow up who are deaf and mute; children with paralysis, with epilepsy, children who have gone mad and crazy due to a trauma; children who suffer from Down's syndrome; children with hydrocephalus or with too small heads; children who are unable or do not want to control their emotions. Children who tend to delinquency already at a young age, children with deformed limbs, feeble-mindedness, stutters, hysterics; all these are children who have been put into this world and who cannot cope with it and therefore hit out in every direction to defend themselves.

Reading the case files of the 180 children who are currently treated in our schools, I hardly find any which describe a normal home; because the family as such is defunct and all other social structures are nothing but a supporting scaffold for an already ruined home.

If these children are to receive help the *first* basic condition for curative education is to bring these children back into a truly social environment. This cannot be an institute or a school with dormitories and classrooms, with a dining hall and every other perceived requirement of a so-called institute, where teachers come and go and nurses and assistants and doctors have their work times and disappear again, leaving the child to his own devices. Everyone, educators, teachers, assistants, nurses, doctors, can only help if they live with the children and do this whole-heartedly. If they form a family group with the children and if their own families are part and core of this family group.

Only then will the child subconsciously experience, 'Now I am at home.' Death and anxiety will not loom at every corner waiting to strike.

For this reason we have distributed the children here in Camphill into as many houses as possible (eleven at the moment) where each child is 'at home.' The kitchen, the playroom, the classroom, the bedrooms belong to them, the children. They help with every necessary task as best they can, in the house, in the garden, in the grounds, with the hens, in the kitchen.

Every adult, however, who lives and works with the children and educates them needs to develop parental feelings for these children; these adults need to understand that nowadays it is necessary to create new families which are not based solely on blood relationships and heredity but on the intention to help and love these children who have actually become 'parentless.' Because although these children have a father and a mother, they have separated themselves from their families because of their illnesses and aberrations, and now need this new family which is created on the strength of the intention to help.

To give the assistants and teachers, nurses and carers the strength required for this task a community of all those who work in these institutes and schools needs to be formed. This community, however, can only be a spiritual community which from within strives towards a goal which everyone as an individual, and at the same time as a community with their brothers and sisters, tries to achieve. The ideological and religious unity of such a community is the basis for the new family which forms the social backbone for these children.

In Camphill we have tried to solve this principal issue by making the community, which strives to stimulate the most positive strengths in the people who belong to it, the core of the social structure. Everyone who lives and works in the schools and institutes is part of it.

Pursuing curative education without putting this primary social insight into practice will always result in doing things by halves; such a curative education will be helpful for individual children but it will ignore the basic problem.

This basic problem is that the social order has broken down; as a result there is an alarming increase in children who need curative education because the structures within which children could hitherto grow up have disintegrated. New structures need to be created and formed so that these children find their feet again.

The collapse of the social order results in children growing up who show all kinds of disorders, inhibitions, deformations and aberrations. These symptoms, which express themselves in such cases, are seen as something commonly described as abnormal or pathological. These terms, although plain enough, are not justified. Because these children do not show anything abnormal or special which otherwise does not exist, but they simply display something that otherwise is hidden within the normal child.

If someone playfully takes a clockwork out of its case and takes the cogs apart, something is lying visibly in front of him which is normally concealed. In the same way an otherwise concealed inner element of a difficult child becomes visible. There is nothing new, nothing has been added, instead something concealed has become apparent.

Because the social order, the case, is broken, the form of the human being is also broken as a consequence; the inner structural and formative principles of the 'image of the human being' reveal their inside and the pathological children are the expression of this.

All human beings bear the formative principles of hydrocephalus, microcephalus, giantism or dwarfism within themselves. All of us have the tendency to epilepsy, paralysis, disability, deafness or blindness. Somehow all of us have the tendency of being a hysteric, criminal or kleptomaniac. Only because these tendencies and potentials are kept in balance they do not show themselves as something apparent.

For example, as an embryo or infant every human being is potentially hydrocephalic. In proportion to the rest of the body the head is far too big and only by gradually overcoming this tendency does the person grow from being an infant to becoming a child of school age. Not overcoming this tendency, however, will result in the distinct condition of hydrocephalus.

But if this tendency which slowly transforms the large head of the infant into to a head in proportion to the growing body of the school child, if this tendency is too strong or sets in too early the result will be a small-headed, microcephalic child.

For example, in the morning, when waking up from sleep, we are all potential epileptics with the tendency of waking up too deeply within our body organization and thus producing an epileptic fit. Fear, shock and fright can do the same.

Knowing this with your heart, in fact, belongs to the *second* basic foundation of curative education. It is the curative educator's attitude of the heart which needs to be present at all times. Because the teacher needs to know that in himself, in every human being, the same tendencies exist which are evident in the child he is supposed to educate. The curative educator needs to identify those aberrations within the child which also exist as powers in the body, soul and mind of every human being but which have started to take excessive effect within the child in his care. In addition to this the teacher also needs to be able to experience within himself the polar tendency which prevented him from developing hydrocephalus, epilepsy, kleptomania or muteness.

If he acquires such an inner aptitude that when he encounters each child he instinctively identifies with the aberrations of his pupil, in a way imitating him inwardly and thus generating the healing powers within himself, then just encountering the child will be of help.

But if in addition he can derive from this inner experience a particular educational intervention through which he can support the child's own motivation for healing, then he will be a true curative educator.

He will then realize that children with a hydrocephalic tendency should draw instead of paint; because they need inner contours and shapes. Children with microcephaly, however, need to paint on broad surfaces so that their tendency of rigidity begins to loosen.

When teaching an epileptic child the teacher will feel the constant need to protect him from drowning in his corporality, to keep the child light and floating, which can be achieved when the true educator consistently directs the child's attention to something new and thus steadily turns him into a sanguine person.

But if he has to teach a pupil with concentration problems he needs to condense the learning material to a degree that it acts like ballast; that it counteracts the child's flighty tendency like a stone weighing down in the child's memory so that the ability to remember is consciously formed.

This type of instruction cannot simply be thought up. It needs to have its source in active practice and should arise in the moment of teaching. The curative educator's greatest virtue is presence of mind. For this reason Rudolf Steiner advised us to become 'dancers.' 'Can't you become dancers?' he asked his listeners in the Curative Education Course.

But this becoming a 'dancer' in the sense of Nietzsche requires the most intimate inner schooling. It does not mean to become a captor or rogue, a joker, who conceitedly puts himself in the limelight in front of the children. The curative educator needs to do one thing: constantly and on a daily basis he needs to engage himself in the true image of the human being which is an image of divine creative power. Only in this way will he obtain this inexhaustible source of presence of mind in class.

Therefore the second basic foundation of curative education

is formed when the true image of the human being guides the educator in all his actions so he can continuously apply remedial interventions to the children in his care.

The third element which forms the basis required for curative education is the medical work of the doctor. This, however, is not about curing acute or chronic diseases but about bringing the principles of medicine as a whole to their effect.

An acute disease exposes the human being to a sudden change within his living space, the body.

In chronic diseases these changes within the living space are mostly the result of his own emotional-mental shortcomings.

In the child with curative-educational needs the cause of the disruption lies much deeper because here the image of the human being has been shifted and dislocated in its very foundations and therefore modern medicine finds it so difficult to integrate the curative-educational field into its discipline. Nobody knows what curative education actually belongs to. Is it part of education? Part of medicine?

Rudolf Steiner left no doubt about it and placed curative education as a whole within the Medical Section of the School of Spiritual Science.

Because here the doctor has a very particular task associated with his relationship to the child with behavioural problems. In this case he is completely a healer, because here the basic gestures of the image of the human being he encounters are deformed and therefore obvious, and so he is constantly required to observe what is broken and disintegrated. And in the future childhood teratology and psychopathology will be cornerstones of medical learning as a matter of course.

In the same way as the clock maker can only learn from the dismantled clock how it works, the doctor can only gain an understanding for what is normally concealed if he studies what is visible and fully developed.

But how is it possible to heal what is broken? That is, how can the art of healing counteract the breakdown of the image of the human being through various medications?

Here the analogy of the image of the human being as a microcosm is required. In the natural world the human being represents its beginning and end. What has evolved in the natural world is incorporated in the human being. He bears mineral, plant and animal within himself. The changing seasons, spring and autumn, summer and winter, are part of his nature. The course of the planets and the stars is inscribed in him and the powers of the sun and the moon also have their effects in his substance.

In an argumentative way of thinking you could say that animals, plants and stones are the difficult children of man and that curative education has failed them. They represent the image of the human being that has broken up into its various parts.

But in its parts, the basic formative tendencies are more strongly represented than in the human being himself. They only need to be identified.

When I see a cuttlefish squirting dark liquid at every disturbance of its biological balance and thus hiding from the world behind a cloak of ink and withdrawing, I can see that the same type of reaction also exists in ourselves in a situation when we want to conceal ourselves from the environment.

I remember a child who suffered from constantly recurring petit mal seizures into which he fled from his environment. The child's skin was covered in a dry, chapped eczema and hardened as a result; it was as if the child was living inside a shell. Sepia, the medication extracted from the liquid ejected by the cuttlefish, proved to be of vital help for this child.

If the doctor has the opportunity to examine the signature of the animals, plants and stones, that is to study the inner formative powers, the special tendencies of the separated parts of the image of the human being, then he will also be able to apply healing interventions in the child with behavioural problems.

Limestone and silica, for example, represent two basic therapeutical medications. When the light of thought and senses is not bright enough, silica will be helpful; but if intentional and creative powers are too feeble and tired, limestone will prove to be of help.

What curative eurythmy and art eurythmy can potentially achieve if effectively introduced to therapy as lyre play and singing, should not be overlooked. For example, here in Camphill we were able to successfully encourage hearing and speaking in deaf-mute children within a year just by doing simple eurythmy and musical exercises for an hour on a regular daily basis; in these cases the power of musical resonance has activated the sleeping energies of the soul.

This, however, leads to the conclusion that the doctor's attitude in curative education requires one thing: the unconditional commitment of the doctor. He needs to be courageous enough to constantly attempt to make the impossible possible. His innermost trust in the power of the medication and his courageous attempts to try and try again form the *third* basic foundation of curative education.

What I have tried to describe here, as I am well aware, is an ideal. But only if we aspire to this ideal will a truly spiritual curative education gradually become a reality.

New social structures need to be developed by the whole community of people living in an institute.

The educator needs to develop those qualities within himself which will help the children in his care.

The doctor needs to understand the natural world in a way that he can match the appropriate medication gained from the natural environment to the pathological tendency in each individual child.

The social family group provides the child with the vital foundation for his existence. His spirit will again feel at home on earth and he will be assured that it is worth his living and working on this earth.

The educator will work to support the child to overcome

what has become too strong or too weak in him. The schooling to which the teacher submits his own soul brings the child's soul the healing comfort it needs.

The body of the child, however, will be guided back from the foundations of his aberrations of destiny to a point where he comes closer to the human vision through the healing substance and the healing word.

So the child with learning difficulties needs:

> the new family for his spirit,
> the true teacher for his soul,
> the good doctor for his body.

Only if these three conditions work together as combined foundations of curative education will thousands of helpless people be helped again, for these children have become an important issue today. They live among us like a problem that is constantly knocking at the gates of human conscience; hence these children are known in western countries as 'the problem children.'

We encounter their being different as the people in ancient Egypt once encountered the sphinx — an ongoing riddle that can only be solved if the question has really been understood. This question, however, is none other than, 'What is the human being?'

7

Modern Curative Education
as a Social Issue

Dear Ladies and Gentlemen!

It really is a very special moment to have the opportunity of speaking here in Hamburg tonight about a problem as important and fundamental as 'Modern Curative Education as a Social Issue.' And right from the start I would like to say that only a few aspects can be touched on, because it is quite impossible to cover such an extensive issue in just one lecture. Still, we need to try to say something about this large present-day problem. At the beginnings of the thirties or at the end of the twenties of this twentieth century a title like 'Curative Education as a Social Issue' would not have been relevant. It may have carried future significance but in those days one could not really speak about curative education as an extensive social issue. This would have been irrelevant and inappropriate. Remembering those years and my own involvement in German curative education, it was all about a limited number of retarded children. You more or less knew which types of retardation you would encounter, and you also knew what the difficulties of children with behavioural problems were — everything arising from the First World War. Something like a social issue with these problematic and delinquent children began to emerge, but this did not exceed the possibilities of education at the time. This has changed radically, because today the number of so-called retarded, disabled, disturbed and handicapped children is ever growing. Whether this number has come about because, for example, improved hygiene has hugely reduced infant mortality is not relevant in the context of this lecture. The total number of children who were described by Rudolf Steiner as in need of soul care is growing and increasing; in some countries at an alarming rate. And it will be necessary not only for doctors, curative educators and the parents concerned, but also for the entire community, especially here in Germany, to take more and more care of this problem.

The last neurologists' congress here in West Germany in September of this year [1963] focused on the issue of the developmentally retarded child. Professor Clemens Benda, who is well known and has a significant role in curative education in America, has said with some justification — though statistically this is not fully verified — that in the Federal Republic of Germany we will have to assume a number of approximately 2 360 000 developmentally retarded children and young people. This is an enormous number if you consider that two million of them are those who need special education, and that 360 000 are those who have not yet been given some degree of education because they are still described as ineducable — not just difficult to educate. If you also assume that, for example, a very thorough estimate conducted by some parents' and doctors' associations in the USA last year showed that five million retarded, disabled, disturbed children and young people live there, you can begin to realize what this problem means for the United States, particularly if you consider that of these five million only half a million are really being taken care of. This means that for the time being four and a half million have to live their dire existence in their families without education, care, or protection. The purpose of their lives is living death because nobody is doing for them what should be done. This is such a common phenomenon that today you have to assume that in each civilized country 12–14 per cent of the children are retarded. In Sweden this number is even higher. This is one side of the situation; the other side is the following.

Since the end of the Second World War people's conscience for the retarded child has awoken. This was an immediate, widespread process in Britain, in America, in Holland, in Scandinavia and during the last few years also here in Germany. Parents' associations have been formed; the biggest one in America, for example, has 900 000 members. If you think of what Lebenshilfe (the association to support people with intellectual disabilities) here in Germany has already achieved during the few years of its existence, you will realize that this is really about an awakening of conscience. In Great Britain, for example, we have a new law for retarded adults and children because comprehensive legislation was passed in Parliament in 1959. This legislation is about turning things around. It aims at gradually lifting the exclusion of retarded and mentally ill people and endeavours to reintegrate many or most of them into human society again. This is a huge step forward. Not excluding them, not taking them out of human community, but taking them back according to their potential. This shows us what is relevant today regarding this issue. And if you also consider that President Kennedy, in his New Year address to Congress, saw it necessary to refer to the problem of the retarded child and the retarded person as one of the most important problems in America, you will understand that it is justifiable today to speak about curative education as a social issue. It is also the case that a great number of scientists, educators, psychologists, physicians, geneticists and biochemists have begun research in this area. The literature on this subject has now become so extensive that it is hardly possible to keep track of each individual study and every result. This gives you a general picture of the situation today.

The misery of retarded children cannot be kept quiet any longer. The awakening of the past fifteen or twenty years has been too powerful. Thousands and thousands of people actively work — not just in theory — on this issue. It is the problem Rudolf Steiner had already referred to as a social issue in 1922, 1923 and 1924. He pointed out that in the conditions of retarded people something appears which we cannot find in what are called 'normal' people and that we need to pay great and urgent attention to this. We shall return to this later.

Over and over again you hear the following question, 'Can you actually tell us why it is that the number of retarded children today is growing to this extent, that retarded children not only grow in numbers but that there are completely new types of retardation — non-contact, psychopathy, schizophrenia — in developing children?' Is there an answer for this? This is a for-midable question and I do not think that there is just one answer. Numerous factors play into this. Apart from this, however, there is a second question, 'If this is the situation, what can we actually do? What do we have to do in order to stem this tide?' You can imagine that I have thought about this question of 'why' and 'what can we do,' that here and there, in various countries of the world, I have tried to find an answer. Every answer to such a complex question is by necessity one-sided. But I think that there is one fundamental answer, an answer that may perhaps provide the base for finding more: It is that our present civiliza-tion is a civilization of adults, of grown-up men and women, but not a civilization of children.

These are harsh words but I think they are true. For our chil-dren — and with this I mean *all* children (and I am not blaming anyone, I am just trying to give a factual description) — there is no place in our civilization, nor is there time for our children, nor is there any understanding for our children which comes from the heart. I am of the opinion that with the advent of the industrial age, with the advent of the industrial revolution (and we shall still speak about this) this characteristic of the present time became more and more evident and distinctive. With this I do not mean that there is not a great deal being done for children today — playgrounds are being built, housing schemes are designed in such a way that children can live there again, and the youth welfare services do all sorts of things to give children a place to go. But just this is a sign of the fact that as a matter of course, in their immediate situation, children have no place, there is no time for children, children have to grow up among us without the experience of being understood from the heart.

I will give you a few examples for this. For the last fifteen years we have noticed the phenomenal acceleration in the growth of children and young people. This means that today our children grow and mature much faster than before, and they not only grow and mature faster, but they also grow much taller than ever before. Many of you, perhaps most of you, know alarming examples; for instance that today a child at the age of four is as far developed as formerly a child was at the age of six or seven, and — I am not exaggerating — girls nowadays menstruate at the age of ten or eleven whereas twenty-five years ago they did so at the age of thirteen or fourteen. If I then also give you the example of Finnish and Swedish girls who, at the start of this century, used to have their first menstruation at the age of seventeen or eighteen and now have it at the age of twelve or thirteen you will realize what this is about. The time of youth, childhood, is getting shorter so that there is not enough time left to be a child, to be young. This has not been brought about by teachers alone, this has not been brought about by parents. This has been brought about by this civilization which is basically a civilization of adults which — because it lacks understanding — does not want children to experience their childhood, their existence as such, their being human among us and with us.

Today a child in England who hopes for further education is required to sit an exam at the age of eleven. This exam at the age of eleven determines at this early stage which special subjects the child is going to take. In Rhineland-Westphalia, Germany, the exam tasks of a high-school graduate — and here I quote from a report of one of the leading pediatricians, Professor Hellbrügge in Munich — have specialized questions which are almost on a par with medical science. Hellbrügge argues that twenty years ago such questions were not appropriate even in medical state examinations. Seventeen-year-old girls had to answer a question referring to erythroblastosis, or the Rh factor, to pass their exam. Imagine this, and also consider that parents are happy with this and continue to push their children into learning ever more material. Or for example, think about the current experiment started last spring in the small town of Georgetown, Pennsylvania, where the director of local education set the school age to start at the age of 3½. In Georgetown 3½ year old children have to attend school regardless of their parents' wishes. This experiment is a government intervention being carefully evaluated by all the pre-set assumptions of American statistics, and if in three or four years time it proves to be successful it will be rolled out across the whole of the United States. I mention this to describe the tendencies. The tendency of our present civilization which denies children their childhood. Our present civilization wants children to grow up as soon as possible, to find their way into so-called life as fast as possible, without knowing that being a child, being young, being human does not mean to specialize but to be of a general nature.

This is surely the great positive trait of Waldorf education — that it develops the child's general nature as long as possible because specialization will set in early enough anyway. What do our children of today play with? Where do our children nowadays have the opportunity to experience nature? Where, for example, has our understanding of a child from the heart gone? By this I do not mean that children are clean, that goes without saying; that they are clothed, that is a matter of course; that they are fed well, that too should be taken for granted. But that the child, the human being, the son, is understood by the father, that the daughter is understood by the father, that the parents spare the time, that they sit down with the child, that they talk to him, that they take a walk with the child, that they celebrate together, that they pray together — where do you still find this? This is what I mean: that our civilization of today is under pressure from circumstances (and again, I am not blaming anyone, merely describing) and has no place, no time, no understanding from the heart.

The consequence of this is that children who are emotionally and mentally not strong enough, who are born with developmental deficiencies, who from the start do not have the chance of asserting themselves emotionally and mentally, these children break under the pressure of this not-being-there-for-them, this not-having-time, this being-pushed. I cannot tell you in how many cases I have witnessed a child at the age of twelve or even at eleven breaking down under the pressure of circumstances, how young people do not even have the option of resisting this pressure, how they flee at the age of eleven, ten or nine into psychopathology, into mental illness — and they really do flee. If they do not receive special help in time this life will be wasted in some sort of aberration and obliteration. It is this lack of understanding from the heart, an understanding of what a young person, a child, still carries within himself and what we call the image of the human being, which all of us carry within ourselves.

This is just the context of present-day curative education. It is no longer solely a matter of dealing with these so-called abnormalities. Today it is a matter concerning all the children in our civilization and this also includes all the parents, because due to their lack of understanding parents do things which can only be described as sick and absurd.

This, however, is related to another important issue crucial to the whole context of our problem. It is today's changing family structures. During the past seven or eight years extensive studies have been conducted in this field by various experts here in Germany. For example, there is the book by Wurzbacher, a professor in Kiel. In far-reaching surveys of German families he was able to establish that this change has been brought about because the family structure which 150 years ago was described as an extended family no longer exists. Not that I wish to sing a song of praise for the extended family as such; I just want to describe a fact. Did you know that, for example, at this time only 50 per cent of all Germans were married at some point in their lives compared to 95 to 96 per cent nowadays? This, too, is no criticism but just a statement that has relevance. In those days extended families also included farm labourers and maids, apprentices, journeymen and servants. Cousins, aunts, grandmothers and great-aunts, everyone was together in a big household. Amidst all this children usually had an excellent life. This has disappeared. Today there is the nucleus family, there is a need for it to be there, and the nucleus family consists of parents and children.

About ten years ago new housing was built near Bristol, small family homes, delightfully situated, with all conveniences. Those who had lived in the slums of Bristol were invited to live there. Within two years 40 per cent of those who lived in the new housing suffered emotionally; many needed psychiatric treatment, others became nervous or anxious. The simple reason for this was that in the new surroundings the growing nucleus family did not have enough substance, especially among simple people. The grandmothers, fathers, aunts no longer lived nearby, the mother could no longer go to her parents' house around the corner. Instead a new, completely self-reliant family unit was supposed to establish itself.

Today approximately 14 per cent of German families are still managed in a patriarchal way. In these families there are still religious principles, the father is the master in the house, and the mother and children have little to say. In another 12 per cent of families the father still *wants* to be a patriarch but the children and particularly the mother doubt his capacity. Then there is a large number of families, 72 per cent, in which husband and wife try to be equal partners and genuinely try to build a family together. This is a sign of a change of family structures which basically points in the right direction. But Wurzbacher concludes at the end of his studies (I cannot quote this word for word but I can accurately paraphrase) that fathers and mothers today do not yet have adequate parenting skills. This is nothing new, we are aware that we are on the right track.

But this change within family structures is the very background to what I have described as having 'no time,' 'no place,' 'no understanding from the heart' for children. Now children grow up who — due to some kind of deficiency, some kind of inner weakness, some kind of inner helplessness and loss of stability in this as yet unstructured nest, due to their parents' not-yet-being-capable, due to their parents' resistance to tackling the immediate task with the child — develop all sorts of conditions. And now it is essential to realize how these children hold a mirror up to parents and adults.

That which in ourselves, in all of us, can still be kept within the range of normality, which we just manage to keep under control without letting it slip into aberration, this becomes a reality in our children. Our children are our judges; not condemning judges, but judges who hold up the mirror to ourselves.

Think about the thalidomide disaster. The child bears a fate which has been generated by the mothers, doctors and fathers. And this is just one of the many examples we constantly see today. What actually are the children with so-called contact disorders? What actually are the so-called psychopaths, the schizophrenics whose intellect is basically completely normal and who still do not have the ability of communicating with other people, other children, other objects, other beings? Do you know that the number of these children is growing at an alarming rate? Do you know that, for example, in America special institutes need to be opened particularly for these children because their number is increasing all the time? And people are still unaware of what this means because they avoid facing the truth that our own inability to have social contact, which we just manage to cover up and conceal, becomes a visible fact in our children. These children are there, right in front of us, not

103

as something separate from everybody else, but they are there in front of us and demand the right to further education, the right to everything which other children too may regard as their right.

And this leads us now to our second question, 'What do we need to do? What can we do? Is it possible to take decisive steps in this situation?'

This points in two directions. First of all we need to acquire a true understanding of these children. Because despite all the new studies, discoveries and interventions we have made in this field, the basic attitude of doctors and laymen, psychologists and many ordinary people towards these children is often still wrong. Old, ancient ideas of sin still exist in the context of these children. It is only a few weeks ago that a Protestant minister, a very progressive minister, an extraordinarily talented, young minister complained to me. In the big institute under his management he said, 'Do know what I have to overcome above all? My carers' attitude. They are still convinced that one is not allowed to do anything for these children as God has given them to us in the form and way they are, and it is seen as a sin if we want to help them!' We can still hear this kind of thing in Germany in 1963.

This is not an isolated comment. In South Africa, for example, during my first years of work there, I had extraordinary difficulties explaining to some parents that these children should not be hidden away. That they are not a sin, that they do not represent an ordeal but that it can be a blessing for parents to have such children because due to these children they will rise to tasks which parents of normal children do not have.

Not far from this antiquated concept is the idea that such children are always brought about by genetic failure. One idea is antiquated-religious, the other one is — in my opinion — antiquated-scientific. During the past two years Professor Benda, whom I mentioned at the start, has conducted an extensive survey of hundreds of retarded children and adults in an institute in Connecticut, and he has gleaned the following result: that at most 5 to 10 per cent of retarded people are in some way affected by genetic disorders. Knowing this, and not only *knowing* this but really *understanding* it, is an enormous step forward. We can then abandon the idea that this is hereditary and therefore you cannot do anything about it. The fact is, it is not hereditary but there are many more influences, circumstances and conditions which result in retardation, illness, imbecility, disability.

We as doctors really had to learn this lesson over the past fifteen to twenty years. We have learnt to pay attention to the fact that, for example, a trauma during pregnancy can result in severe conditions of intellectual retardation in children; that an illness at a very early age, that an illness of the mother during the second and third month of pregnancy can result in all kinds of severe abnormalities. I could probably tell you about hundreds of examples where a trauma of the child, a trauma of the mother, an illness of the mother or an emotional disturbance of the mother during pregnancy brought about all kinds of aberrations in the child. If you take this as a reality, and do not just write it down in order to add it to your knowledge, but if you begin to make it the source of your actions then you understand that all these children, or most of them, are basically normal. A trauma, an accident, a genetic failure have condemned these normal children to cope with this insult.

Here you encounter another prejudice which frequently comes to the fore. There is indeed the general impression — and most people are still convinced of this — that these children are different from others because they are less or not at all 'intelligent.' This is one of the worst misunderstandings you can find in this field! What actually is intelligence?

Intelligence surely is not just intellect, for every intelligence assessment, every intelligence test we conduct is in fact based on a whole range of emotional skills: memory, emotions, capacity to act, social adjustment. All this is actually part of intelligence. It is not the case that these children are stupid or idiots; far from it. I have never, not a single time, seen a truly hereditary disability but I have seen many cases of acquired disability which have often been brought about by a wrong diagnosis or wrong treatment. Inappropriate treatment of such a child leads to a gradually increasing disability. The intellectual potential of the child was not reduced but rather the abilities of the child and the opportunity to let the child's potential intelligence thrive and develop within his environment. This does not mean in any way that each child can be helped. It would be inappropriate to make such a claim. However, I am convinced that we could bring many more children back into a practical-active life, into a human and individual existence, if we accepted these children in good time, without any prejudices, the way they are: that is, as children like every other child, as a human being like every other human being with a right to education, with a right to treatment, with a right to guidance and protection. And in saying this I am already talking about the basic foundations of all curative education because the foundations of all curative education are fourfold.

First of all we need to learn to diagnose these children accurately. Idiocy, imbecility, debility belong to a nomenclature which may be of some meaning to civil servants, or even to civil servants dealing with education. To children and parents, to curative educators and teachers they do not mean anything. They are like judges' verdicts. But every child has the right to be assessed over weeks and months in order to find out why he is paralysed or retarded, why he cannot speak, why he behaves in a strange manner, why his feet, fingers or hands do not grow, why he has difficulty moving, why he cannot keep up with the further stages of child development. On this diagnosis all further assessment and treatment is based.

In fact, each of these children can be treated individually with curative education. This was first described by Rudolf Steiner and his explanations, which have been developed further, are also based on this. This is the second foundation, that each child can receive individual treatment using colour and sound, movement, gymnastics, eurythmy, all kinds of interventions.

What I am going to tell you is solely based on my own experience. It is about the principles according to which we have established our schools in the Camphill movement. Each child has a right to being taught and if I say 'being taught' I mean being taught in class. In Camphill children are sent to school according to their age. According to the Waldorf curriculum they not only learn reading, writing and numeracy but also history, geography, science, foreign languages and music, everything that children usually learn. All children take in the learning material, many of them understand it, some of them can reproduce it and if they do so then these children gradually reintegrate into the general process of human history. Because the knowledge of the past which we convey to our children, our fathers' and forefathers' achievements, this is what our children are supposed to carry on. Since we have introduced this educational programme in all our residential schools in the last twelve years our children, as retarded as they may be, appear in the amazing light of being children, show confidence and integrate in all social events. This is the third foundation!

And the fourth foundation is simply the soul care and hygienic care appropriate to each child. Keeping children with developmental deficiencies in big institutes is not appropriate any more. And do not say we don't have enough staff! Rather say we don't have enough understanding, we don't have enough commitment, we don't have enough enthusiasm to engage the many people who want to help. You cannot entrust a deaconess with forty severely ill children and think that you have solved the problem. With this you have only done what otherwise is also done in cowsheds, that is, to make sure that there is a certain degree of food and cleanliness. This leads to hospitalization in such children, this leads to regression, this leads to disability.

Only one of the basic foundations described here cannot help alone, only curative education, only diagnosis, school alone will not be able to help. Real curative education for children and young people is based on these four pillars. Then real help may be possible — it will be insufficient and full of errors — but it will be possible. In Camphill 30 to 35 per cent of these children are led back into a normal life. The others stay on. And for those others further interventions are required because they, too, cannot be just shunted off somewhere. I would like to mention the attempts we have made over the last years.

Acknowledging all the extraordinarily positive efforts regarding sheltered workplaces (which, for example, have been established in the Netherlands in an exemplary way) we have tried to take this a step further. We came to the question, what do these young adults, who cannot go out into the world, need to create their own life? What is required for a grown-up, retarded person, whether he is Down's syndrome or postencephalic, a psychopath, suffering from contact disorder or epilepsy or something else? What do they all have in common, what is it that they really lack? The answer is that none of them is able to master their own destiny. That is, they are not capable of finding their own career, to pursue this career and to use their earnings to create an individual, secure life or to start a family. This is where we need to begin. We actually need to do what they cannot do. We need to give them the environment within which they can become what they are meant to be.

Eight years ago these questions led us to the following conviction: These people need three defining social elements which are also needed by all of us, by every one of us. The first element is a *family*. The second is *work* (and if I say work I mean work and not just being kept busy). And the third element is the opportunity of *social inclusion*. We then set about to try and provide these people with these elements. Together with the parents we built a kind of village. A village community was developed in which small family groups are formed for these young men and women (as they are no longer children) where they form small groups together with their foster parents, a family unit not based on blood relations but on spirituality. Secondly, within such village communities, we have tried to create workshops as well as farms and market gardens where they can work. The third element is to devise such village communities in such a way that they are governed by social respect for the human being so that there is mutual acknowledgment, appreciation, the capacity to learn and personal growth. It is safe to say that this experiment has been successful.

Our first village which we established eight years ago, in 1955, where now a hundred so-called villagers live and work in twelve small households, this village is now also an economic innovation. We produce toys, cut glassware, wax candles for general shops (not just for charity stalls); we have a weavery, a large nursery garden; a bakery; a big joinery where toys are made. Everything is sold on the general market and brings in so much money that, together with the Deficiency Grant which we receive regularly from the Department of Employment, it nearly covers all the running costs. In this way these villagers largely contribute to their financial support. From the start we have arranged for no care allowance to be paid for them, neither by the government nor by the parents, so that it becomes a matter of course for them to recognize: this is *our* community, *we* organize it, *we* are responsible for it. Each of these people can do that. I could mention quite a number of exemplary things. For example, during these eight years these young brothers and sisters who live together in small households have never shown any sexual misconduct. Some of these young people have married and these relationships are extraordinarily good and right. If you have the chance of visiting such a community you will have difficulty telling who are the so-called normal people and who are the so-called abnormal ones.

Today there are already such village communities in England, Scotland, Ireland, the United States, South Africa and

Switzerland. I hope that here in Germany you will soon have a village where these young adults will not only be looked after but where they can work and lead their true, real life in decency.★

In some of these communities we could arrange that a priest of the Christian Community lives there permanently. I would wish for everyone to participate in the Act of Consecration of Man during which, for example, the communion is received with a dignity that leaves one moved to tears. I would wish for everyone to participate in the Bible Evenings on Saturday when these people try to express on the basis of the Gospel what they have encountered and experienced during the course of the week.

So there are places being established where human dignity is given back. And this is what it is all about. But this is a vision of curative education in a narrower sense; and now I would like to talk about curative education in a broader sense.

Such places, homes and village communities should actually be used to a much greater extent. Because there are countless people who drop out from the rush and the bustle of life, and no longer know how to go on or where to go. We know, for example, about the big problem of the care for the elderly. Grandmothers and grandfathers have become separated from the family unit because the extended family no longer exists. As a result care homes for the elderly need to be built. This provides these people with a roof over their heads, it gives them the opportunity of living with others. And yet there are many who want more. There are so many who would still like to take on responsibility. It is a wonderful opportunity to have a house with four or five elderly people connected with a curative educational community where some of them take the children for a walk, another one has her own foster child who has no parents and for

★ In 1964 this wish came true with the foundation of the village community at the Lehenhof.

whom she cares, where they can celebrate together, where they can knit or sew for the children. I am frequently asked, 'And what do you do with your staff once they are old, where do they go?' Their place is within our communities; because there they can be at home again. There they are not required to do regular work, but can live in a way that allows them to participate in many things from which otherwise elderly people are excluded.

Then there is a number of young people who in today's times have lost their orientation. I know many of them who, by encountering retarded children and adults, have developed what had been lacking until then: active compassion and love. Why do we miss such opportunities? Indeed we should not organize everything so that it results in specialization, but we should allow life to take its course as broadly and generally as possible. The so-called retarded people can be the ones who initiate healing in our modern social life if only we let them, if we had a sufficiently vivid imagination to see that they are people who also matter. In fact, in these people something is much more obvious than in the so-called normal ones, and this is the eternal human. In each of them something of the specific nature of being a child has not yet been buried, this nature which is apparent in the artist or the young child. And this what is needed today. In this way, being a retarded person is not seen as a negative thing, it is seen as a divine gift brought into this civilization. A Down's syndrome child is a source of love and joy who can give us back things we all have lost. And this can be done by hundreds of people.

Let us allow them to do what they can do, let us give them the opportunity to express themselves so that we receive their help and they ours. Because it is truly the case that they who were the least, can become the very first of a future social life — if we really want this.

Karl König and three boys, Italy 1964.

8

Curative Education as a Social Task

Ladies and Gentlemen,

It is a very special honour for me to be able to speak to you in this house; because this means that my life's work has generated interest and has contributed to the fact that leading figures of public life are beginning to support curative education.

This evening, however, I do not want to talk about the Camphill movement, but would like to say something about curative education as a social task in general; to describe something that has evolved from nearly 35 years experience of living and working together with retarded people, with mentally handicapped children, with people with disabilities, actually with all those who have difficulty establishing themselves as a person on earth.

If one had the intention of speaking about modern curative education as a social issue during the twenties only a few would have known what was meant by this. Because basically curative education was not a social issue in those days. In those days there were mentally handicapped adults and mentally handicapped children. They still could to some extent be integrated into society and the state as a whole. Then momentous events swept over the earth. The Second World War broke out and after it had ended, when people thought that there were far more important issues to solve and to deal with, all of a sudden it seemed as if the conscience of humanity, particularly of

civilized humanity, woke up to the question of curative education as a social issue.

This has become a very broad problem. It is one of the most
obvious problems of our time, not only because the number of
these children and people has risen continually, one could say to
an alarming degree, but it has also become a social issue because
there has been a sudden incidence of the most various forms of
retardation and disability as well as new kinds of childhood psychopathy. These are conditions and behaviour which were
unknown twenty-five or thirty years ago. In those days you may
have encountered them in a few isolated cases. But now there is
a whole army, not just of thousands but of tens of thousands of
autistic children in America, England and Scotland; there is
another huge army of post-encephalitic children spreading
across the whole of Europe, America, South Africa, etc. These
are completely new phenomena. If you fail to consider this, then
you have no idea what the question of curative education as a
social issue really is about.

Last year in the United States of America a parents association, which is the equivalent of your Lebenshilfe association,
conducted a statistical survey to record the number of children
and young people in need of care. The result was an estimated
number of five million. So there are five million disabled,
retarded, psychopathological, etc. children and young people in
the United States today. This is alarming enough. Far more
alarming, however, is the fact that of these five million only half
a million receive the kind of care, education and guidance which
would be appropriate for them; this means that 90 per cent of
these children and young people have to live their lives in their
families or other circumstances without appropriate care.

The last neurologists' congress held here in Germany focused
on the problem of disability. On that occasion the well known
professor, Clemens Benda, who manages a big research institute
in Connecticut, said that in his opinion it should be assumed
that there are approximately 2 360 000 retarded and disabled

children and young people here in the Federal Republic of Germany.

These are not totally accurate numbers but they are a kind of indicator of the extent to which the problem has grown today. If you take into account that of these 2 360 000 children about 2 000 000 can be *educated* in special schools, in schools for children with learning difficulties, but that the remaining 360 000 are still — and in my opinion completely unjustifiedly — described as 'ineducable,' then you will be able to understand or have an idea of how wide-ranging a problem this is.

This is by no means a German or American, an English or Scottish problem. It is a *global* problem. It seems as if something is emerging within humanity whose scope and extent has not been experienced until now. It is a huge army of people who have appeared and challenged us. And we have to be honest with ourselves about the fact that at present we are insufficiently prepared to meet the challenge.

But this is what it is all about! You could ask, 'What shall we do now?' Everything we have tried to do before was merely an attempt to scratch the surface of these phenomena, but we have not yet really explored the depth of the problem. We have not yet even tried to reflect on this problem in depth, and from our reflections grasp what we can and need to do.

But if we ask, 'What can we do?' we need to consider first in which area curative education as a social issue needs to be approached. Today there are, for example, parents' associations in most civilized countries. Here you have your Lebenshilfe, in Britain there is the big National Society of Parents of Handicapped Children, in America, in Canada and other countries there are similar institutions.

Above all these associations aim to alleviate the distress of mothers as well as the distress of the families concerned in order to prevent these people being overwhelmed. This is an important aspect and you need to consider this; but you should be aware that this is indeed only *one* aspect. The purpose of these institutions is to *help* the families affected. For this reason day care centres for children are created; recreational and holiday homes are established. Sheltered workshops are set up to relieve mothers and families and to provide the children with an activity and an environment where they are no burden to their family, and are not at risk of simply turning inwards. This is the answer for *one* requirement; but indeed it is just *one* answer and one should be wary of believing that such institutions are the whole solution to this social problem.

Furthermore we are facing another problem which concerns us, especially in Britain. It is the question, 'How can retarded, disabled and psychopathic people, who were excluded until now, be reintegrated into society, into everyday life?'

The first and foremost purpose of Britain's new Mental Health Bill, which was passed into legislation by Parliament in 1959, is to prevent these people being shut away in mental homes and hospitals, and to facilitate the education of the wider public so that all those who are mentally ill, psychopathic, retarded, affected by social deprivation, etc. are encountered in a way that they can be reintegrated into the general stream of human life. For this purpose institutions are being developed. But it will take decades until they really work. Yet it is a start and — in my opinion — an extraordinarily good and positive start. Consequently, however, the part of the population which is still mentally healthy will begin to realize that the ill and retarded are not just abnormal but that they are human beings with their special needs and concerns. That they are sisters and brothers in the same way as the so-called 'normal' people. This is the second answer.

However, the third — and this particularly is an aim of Camphill — is to acquire a new, a real and a true understanding for the disabled, for the retarded, for the psychopathic child. And to glean methods from this understanding through which these children are not excluded but are included in active humanity. These methods provide these children with vital help, giving them the opportunity of being socially integrated and educated to some degree so that they can develop as human beings. We need to become more and more aware of this great task.

Until 1935 most of the spastic children, for example, were regarded as ineducable cripples. They vegetated in their families or in institutions of some description. We do know, since Phelps in America brought these children to our attention and educated us, that through physiotherapy and by responding to the needs of the individual child much can be achieved and much support can be provided. He has shown us that these children are not at all hopeless cripples but that in some cases a lot, in others less and in a few cases hardly anything can be achieved. But that you should work with them, that you should actively support them; this is something all children who suffer from cerebral palsy deserve. This is also true for hearing-impaired, blind and — although at present this is put in practice only in a few places — for *every* retarded and disabled person.

Rudolf Steiner clearly pointed this out in 1924. And since then there are homes where his insights and instructions are applied and tested, and these achievements can only be ignored if one is blinded by prejudice. It is simply a fact that the *child in need of soul care,* as Rudolf Steiner called it, can be educated within certain limits and socially integrated within *wide* limits. It is necessary that today people become increasingly aware of this insight and that it becomes a concern of a big part of the population. We will not achieve anything of significance and we will not even be able to tackle curative education as a social issue if we do not start a campaign to raise awareness focusing on the 'child in need of soul care.'

Let me give you a few examples which I have encountered in Germany over the last few months.

A few weeks ago I received a letter from the mother of a young Down's syndrome infant. She wrote that she had sought advice at a famous university pediatric clinic not far from here. There she was advised to send this child into an appropriate institution and to forget about him since he was just an 'idiot' anyway! This happened in October 1963 here in the Rhineland. Every doctor who nowadays gives such an advice is fundamentally wrong. Because we know how absolutely essential the proximity of motherly love, the love and security of a family is for every infant; whether or not the infant has Down's syndrome is irrelevant and should not make a difference. This is a human being and this human being cannot just be shunted off somewhere because of antiquated ideas. We can no longer afford to tell a mother something as barbaric as this.

The second example is the following story. An extraordinarily well-meaning Protestant minister who, for personal reasons, volunteered to manage a home for retarded children told me the following: 'The biggest problems I have to deal with, I encounter from the side of the carers. Guided by their religious belief these people are utterly convinced that each retarded child is an expression of a divine punishment which has befallen the parents. To help these children would go against God's will.' This is still the view of well-meaning carers in an institute for hundreds of disabled children.

But this is not an isolated example, instead it is an attitude which you encounter frequently. On my lecture tour in South Africa, for example, one of the most important things was to persuade parents, particularly Protestant parents, that it is neither punishment nor sin to have such a child. Subconsciously most of the parents still have a vivid sense that: 'Alas, something has befallen me like a punishment. I cannot actually understand why this has happened to me and not to someone else. What has been my sin?'

In the Protestant home the carers refused to introduce curative-educational interventions because they were afraid that this would interfere with God's will. Well, this is simply religious prejudice. If people do not think of divine destiny they will think of something else. They will think, for example, of genetics and believe that these disorders are mainly a matter of a hereditary disease which we encounter in the form of childhood disability.

Clemens Benda whom I have mentioned earlier conducted an extensive study over the last year during which his scientific assistants examined a few hundred disabled people. The result was that only 5 to 10 per cent of these impairments are caused by genetic failure. This should be inscribed in every curative educator's and pediatrician's heart. Just imagine what it means to parents if you can tell them, 'You *can* have another child! It is *not* the case that the condition is caused by you, by a genetic disorder of you or your family!' And this is true. These conditions have nothing to do with inherited disorders except in very rare cases.

The interesting thing with this is that in the last ten years, and mainly in the last five years, results show that most inherited impairments of these children are generally a matter of metabolism. As a result of this hereditary impairment, the metabolic damage also affects the brain metabolism, thus leading to an inhibited development of the child's personality, thought processes, senses and will.

In the forty years of my curative-educational work I have made one fundamental discovery: basically, there is no such thing as inherited disability. I do not speak these words of great importance glibly. As far as I can see, there is no inherited disability contrary to what is still in dated and antiquated textbooks. Every condition of disability is not inherited but acquired. And this is exactly the trend which is coming more and more to the fore of curative-educational research of the last fifteen years. For each of these children we can identify what has caused a developmental personality disorder or problem if we only examine in detail, if we accurately trace back the child's medical history.

For example, a major statistical study in Glasgow which was conducted three years ago (and I am only mentioning published scientific studies) shows that mothers who, for example, experience a trauma during pregnancy, give birth to a much greater number of retarded and disabled children than is the case with mothers who can go through pregnancy peacefully without any kind of traumatic experiences. There was a time when old people

119

talked about 'mothers' accidents.' This was then increasingly ignored. Now we learn that this wasn't all nonsense and ignorance, but that it really is the case. You often find whenever you speak to mothers, that at one time or another there was a trauma that triggered a mechanism, a biological mechanism, which led to deformation, developmental inhibitions, traumatic effects in the developing child, resulting after birth in something that later manifests itself as disability. This is not due to inheritance, but due to an external or internal attack. I am trying to put this as accurately as possible to show that this is something which only *later* manifests itself as disability. It does not manifest itself from the start but only later, if the child's first years pass without being challenged by helpers and educators to deal with his retardation.

There are, for example, most severe deformities of the ear, the brain, the heart, the eye which until the 1940s were regarded as being hereditary. Today we are absolutely certain that this was simply caused by a flu, rubella or by some other viral infection which the mother had during the second or third month of pregnancy. For the mother this passed almost unnoticed at the time, but it caused consistent trouble for the whole of the child's life.

I mention all this because it is indeed important to consider that such a person, if it hadn't been for this particular incident, would have been born normal. That means that basically these people are complete as a person, but that they are people who at an early stage, while the organs are beginning to develop and ill effects can set in very deeply, suffered the most severe impairments. I think it is important to take this into account as a social issue of curative education when raising public awareness.

And then there is one prejudice that in my opinion belongs to the most significant, to the worst superstitious ideas which affects all of us today when it comes to retarded children and children with behavioural problems. That is, that we think these impairments are defects of intelligence. It is this prejudice that sees the 360 000 children in Germany who are described as more or less 'ineducable,' as indeed suffering from a deficient intellect.

For about forty years I have been living with these children and adults. Many of them do not have the ability to develop their intellect. However, they are prevented from developing their intellect because they do not have the *opportunity* to pursue this intellectual development like a normal child due to certain disorders in their physical or emotional existence. You see, even today people say that Down's syndrome children are just idiots or insensitive. But if you follow the development of a Down's syndrome child and observe accurately, you will find that it is the motor skills which are indeed insufficiently developed.

Because the motor functions of the Down's syndrome child do not fully develop, because such children learn to walk in the second year of life instead of the first, because they only show a slow speech development, that is they begin to develop speech motor control, after the third or fourth or fifth year of life; for these reasons these children continually fail to keep up with their biological and spiritual development, not because they are *stupid,* but because they begin to stand upright too *late,* begin to speak too late, because they do not experience the cognitive development which begins in a normal child at the age of approximately three years.

And if you meet such a Down's syndrome child — and I am not at all telling you anything new here — you will see, this is a full human being already. This is no less a human being than we are, only some of his abilities, and specifically not his intellectual abilities, are different to ours. He is behind in his motor development and therefore his intellect has not developed. And if you study post-encephalitic children you will increasingly notice that in such children the hypo-motor activity, for example, continuously disrupts the flow of thought, the flow of sensory stimuli; that for such a child it is absolutely *impossible* to concentrate.

If we are agitated, if we are stressed and rushed, if we are overwhelmed by emotion, we may be ever so bright, our IQ may be ever so high, but in such circumstances it will be impossible for us to keep a really clear and open mind.

And you see, these things need to be considered now because I am absolutely convinced that it is utterly inappropriate to make a difference between educable and ineducable children. In Britain in a few years' time, the Department of Education will be in charge of *all* children, regardless of IQ. It will be important everywhere, that each child has a right to education.

This morning I had the opportunity of seeing and visiting a model institution of your association in the Ruhr area. For an hour the director and I walked around in this house and in doing so both of us became clearly aware how much can be done for the young ones, and how it is often too late for twelve, thirteen, fourteen, fifteen, twenty, thirty-year-olds.

Here you were able to experience again that disability does not come with a person but that disability only develops if, due to our own incompetence, these children do not receive what they need at the right time and at the right place. And this is one of the biggest social problems we are facing, and this problem cannot simply be tackled with day care centres. I know that at the moment more cannot be done. I know that it is a good thing that at last some kind of start is being made. But if we want to devise a programme for a future curative education, if in perhaps twenty or thirty or forty years' time, within a generation, we want to prevent the tragedy which we are facing in these children *today,* we need to understand that a true curative education can only be put in place if it is based on four pillars. These four pillars are firstly diagnostics, secondly curative-educational therapy, thirdly school and education, and fourthly the home and the family.

Not one, not two, not three but only all *four* interventions can really give the child what protects him from becoming a disabled person.

Firstly about diagnostics. It is a requirement that diagnostic centres are established everywhere. But not diagnostic centres in the form of clinics, because where a diagnostic centre is set up as a clinic, and I know in quite a few of these diagnostic centres, the children's environment is changed in a way that they do not show what they are and what they can be. Above all a diagnostic centre should really only be set up in a way that children are given a *natural* environment where they live over six, eight, ten, twelve weeks in a way that they do not need to be without an intimate family atmosphere, and where, together with two or three friends and in the care of a mother, they spend their time living, playing, sleeping, being awake in homely rooms and doing everything that a child would usually do. The centres must not simply be dormitories where the children are kept clean by nurses and are clinically tested, but where doctors and psychologists are at home in these families in a way that they are able to encounter these children as if they were their own, and as if the observers were close friends and relatives. Only then are the conditions created in which a child appears in his true nature and as he really is.

If you do this differently you will continue to produce new pseudo-diagnoses.

In Camphill it sometimes takes us two to three months to find the right diagnosis for a child. This not only includes an electroencephalogram check, an examination of the child's metabolism, a neurological examination — this is all part of it — but it includes, for example, learning and experiencing how such a child falls asleep, how they wake up, how they behave with other children, what kind of toys they prefer, how they behave in a classroom, how they behave when their parents come to visit. Only then (and it is unnecessary to use statistical methods for everything) will you get a more or less detailed picture of this person. Only then will you notice that there is this or that particular impairment. And basically, as is the case with every true diagnosis, the appropriate therapy is already implied. Such a comprehensive evaluation of the child's nature already implies the curative-educational intervention. Do not think that one or two or three intelligence tests will do. Do not think that an IQ of

75 or 53 represents a diagnosis. This is nothing but a partial symptom.

A diagnosis is the full assessment of a child's personality as it shows itself in more or less normal circumstances.

This is what is required; this is what we need to implement, and only then will it be possible to meet the needs of every child, provided we also do a second thing. And that is from the accurate emotional diagnosis to derive an accurate personality-forming and personality-building curative-educational therapy for each child. Indeed, among the disabled children there are no two alike.

Phelps once said that among ten thousand spastic people he has not seen two who were similar. Each spastic child poses his own problem because each of these children, in common with every human being, is a personality, a fully developed and complete personality. Whether he is intelligent or not, whether he has achieved something in life or not, he is still a personality. And then you can really proceed to therapeutically attend to each of these children individually. This can be done at home as well as in residential homes, schools or residential institutions. Because only if you try, for example by means of motor exercises, playing, drama, music, painting, sculpture, or hundreds of other interventions, to reorganize what is not quite in harmony or what is in great disharmony within each child, then you will begin to do work in a truly curative-educational way.

Of course a lot is already being done through rhythmic exercises and gymnastics. A year ago when I was at a children's clinic in Montreal as an observer, the doctor there demonstrated the following. During the holidays he gathered all the pupils who had difficulties learning in class, and found that they were all behind in motor development. So every day during the holidays for an hour or two he trained these children's motor skills in a very simple, very pragmatic way. He was a very pragmatic person. And you know, the performance of these children rapidly improved after they received thorough physical exercise. Can you imagine what could be achieved if there was eurythmy, if there was curative eurythmy, if there were all kinds of further interventions! This curative educational therapy is the second pillar.

The third one is education in school. In Camphill, in the past twelve years, the approximately 250 children in permanent care have each attended school classes according to their *age*, not to their level of ability, so that the seven-year-olds attend the first class, the eight-year-olds the second class, etc. And they are broadly taught according to the curriculum which Rudolf Steiner devised for Waldorf Schools.

This was one of the most *essential* steps we undertook in Camphill. Because since we have introduced this — and it took many years until we realized how essential such an intervention is — the social integration of these children, the development of these children as human beings has, to express it graphically, shown a steep rise.

I am well aware that some of them cannot reproduce the learning material at all; but all of them can take it in. It is a knowledge which enters the children in an age-appropriate and biologically appropriate way and each of these children knows: I go to school; I sit in class; I learn reading, writing and numeracy, at least to some degree; I participate in history and geography lessons; I learn something about plants and animals; I get an idea of astronomy; I learn a foreign language and therefore reach out to the world. It is indeed absolutely essential that we do not treat these children as stupid, that we do not think they have just limited minds and so there is basically no point in teaching them.

Whoever has joined one of our monthly festivals at the school in Camphill, whoever has heard these children recite in Latin and Greek, in French and German, whoever has seen them performing a short drama — for example, fifteen or sixteen-year-olds performing Shakespeare scenes in a way which conveys that these young people have developed into full human beings —

whoever has experienced all this will begin to understand fully that such an education, even if it only very rarely results in so-called 'normality,' gives these people the opportunity to become who they are.

And this indeed is the task of being human, that every person becomes who he or she is. And if he, as a disabled person, cannot do this alone we need to step in and give him the opportunity, to create conditions of living, education and care that allow this to happen. Education is the third pillar.

The fourth one is concerned with home and care. Ideally, it is preferable by far if these children can stay in their families as far as this is possible. But we all know the practical situations today. Can the majority of these children have a life appropriate to them in their own families? How much does a post-encephalitic child, a disabled child with erethism disrupt family life, how does it affect the siblings? Of course, three, four, five, six hours in a day care centre is better than nothing. Better still is to accommodate these children in a residential school where day and night they can receive the formative interventions, guidance and education needed. A residential school can only achieve this if it is organized like families, that is, if the children live in houses where no more than ten, twelve, fourteen children are together in one house, where they have foster parents day and night so that they can feel safe, secure, sheltered and protected.

These are the four pillars of curative education. In my opinion this is the programme for all future curative education. I am convinced that it will take time to implement it, but it should at least be planned. And it should be understood that the current measures, good as they may be, are by no means enough to achieve the most and the best.

And finally there is one more question. What happens to those who grow up — and there are many who grow up. What should be done with them to avoid their being sent back into institutions or simply 'vegetating' in their families? There are possibilities here. But first let us consider what these young adults are missing in general. They are missing what other young adults can normally do: to choose a profession, to work to the best of their abilities, to learn the necessary skills and to build and create their own life. None of these people have this ability. And for this reason it is essential that we begin to create such an environment for them. We need to give them an environment in which they, without having created it themselves, can live as human beings in their own right.

For this there are two options. Sheltered work places are really only an option for those young adults who still have a supportive family background. If this is not the case, the other option is 'village communities.' We have proved the feasibility of this over the last eight years. Botton Village and other village communities which we started not only function but actually also create a living fabric of social existence for these ill and disabled adults.

Our first project, Botton Village, has progressed so far at present that it is economically and financially viable. None of these young villagers is supported by anyone there. They receive an allowance from the Department of Employment as every other handicapped person does, but that is all. And in the workshops, on the farms, in the gardens, in the bakery, everywhere they work to the full extent of their abilities, so that the products they make are not just sold in charity shops but in general shops, in fully competitive conditions.

Today we produce a vast number of things which cannot be bought elsewhere in Britain or America. And the demand is so great that we struggle to deliver because the things we make are so special, so beautiful and so creative that they bring people joy and gratification.

Just reflect what it means that people who were formerly thought of as not being capable of anything, have come so far that they work in a social village community which they have built themselves, that this work earns them their own living, that they live together in families, that they actually, many of them, even have the possibility of getting married and becoming real citizens.

You see, sheltered workshops are a temporary solution, a necessary temporary solution. However, such village communities can lead further. It was for a reason that the whole of Holland last year collected donations, and within a day they had several million guilders to create such a village, because they had seen that sheltered workshops, which exist in an exemplary way there, are only *one* answer to the problem. A village community is a different answer and such villages should not be conceived in the way that these people are incarcerated and isolated there. This is not at all the case. These are villages, such as other villages, and they communicate with the neighbouring villages in the same way.

And just think what it could mean if, through such institutions, you could take a different direction to solving other problems too. If, for example, you could put a stop to the current rural exodus by educating thousands of these people in such a way that they return from the cities to the countryside. There are always complaints about the shortage of farm workers. Why, indeed, should they not be employed as farm workers, under the guidance of others? This would open completely new opportunities.

Think about the ageing population of today. Vast funds are spent on building care homes for the elderly, yet we know that they are not fully happy in these care homes, because they live together there in an artificial environment where they are no longer aware of the purpose of their life. Why should twenty old people not live in such a village, and help take on these tasks, participating in cultural and other events and finding new friends? All this would be possible if people would just give up this continual specialization.

Ladies and gentlemen, we are surely not made for specialization. We are human beings from top to bottom and not just nuclear scientists or engineers or retarded or disabled people or psychopaths. Only together can people form communities and not those who are segregated. Let us turn away from these dated and completely crazy ideas so that what may become newly established human communities can shine out as an ideal.

This is not about forcing these people into work which is not appropriate for them, this is about much more. This is about the thousands and tens of thousands before us who suddenly, if only we want to see it, reveal what is completely concealed and usually covered, that is the truth of the image of the human being.

Actually, you can only see in a Down's syndrome person, in an epileptic person, in a blind or crippled person what a human being really is because in such a person there still exists what in us has been concealed in thought, prejudice and set ideas by normality.

Let us take these people as one of the greatest positive things we have been given. Let us take them as they are so that they may remind us of their being human and that we may become human again through them. This is the social issue of curative education.

Long ago in Egypt the sphinx stood as a challenge, an enigma, to people. The sphinxes of today are these children who challenge us to stand in front of them and recognize them and in doing so recognize ourselves. This is what it is about. This is not a simple matter of economy, of creed, of party politics. This is the full engagement of a person beyond all these day-to-day things. Then we will find a solution for the social issue of curative education.

The History and Future
of Curative Education

9

Mignon:
The History of Curative Education

1. Introduction

A few years ago, when I made a first attempt to form a concept of the history of curative education, I became aware of the difficulties associated with such a project. Because merely gathering historical information already poses inscrutable obstacles; however, the more one searches for historical dates and facts the more fundamental questions come to the fore which had until then hardly entered the mind: What actually is curative education? At what point is it possible to identify the beginning of a curative-educational movement?

There is no easy answer to these questions; because the historic events in the field of special education and curative education alone do not provide sufficient information. In Britain and America, for example, the term 'curative education' does not exist at all. Although there is a strong, growing curative-educational movement everywhere in the west, a curative education as such is hardly known. A 'child guidance' movement has evolved from child psychology but this is hardly curative education. The major textbooks and journals do not have names which would express a commitment to curative education; for example, the leading American publication is called *American*

Journal of Mental Deficiency, and a leading English textbook by Tredgold is simply called *Mental Deficiency.*

In Germany the term *Heilpädagogik* appeared at the end of the nineteenth century, but I found it impossible to find out at what point it appeared for the first time. This expression emerged in the educational literature and more and more became a term for the special education of children who could not be included in regular schools. Only at the beginning of the twentieth century did schools for children with learning difficulties have their breakthrough and find their place everywhere on earth. Around 1925 there were 1 500 independent special schools doing curative-educational work in Germany alone.

However, this is by no means an answer to the question: What is curative education? Although the curative-educational movement appears in conjunction with the emergence of schools for children with learning difficulties, this does not define curative education as such; apart from the special schools, other areas of youth welfare appear at the same time and really belong to curative education. For example, a whole movement evolved under the name of 'corrective training,' which specially supported children and young people at risk.

But this corrective training had its origins in much earlier attempts to counteract the general misery of children and to prevent some of its worst consequences. The big charity organizations which were founded in the middle of the nineteenth century made it their task to educate neglected children, to give orphans a refuge, to stop child labour in industry, to set up day nurseries and kindergartens, to delay school age, and much more.

At the same time pediatrics emerged as a special field of internal medicine. This is a process which developed over the whole of the nineteenth century and eventually led to the creation of a chair for pediatrics at the University of Berlin in 1926.

The training of certified midwives and baby nurses, the special attention paid to infant mortality, and the appearance of Semmelweiss (1818–65), the Saviour of the Mothers, are further indications of these events. In conclusion, there was a process in all central and western countries during the nineteenth century which can be called an 'awakening to the child.' The rise of industrialization, the associated impoverishment of the middle classes, the emergence of a proletariat and the massive pauperization of large parts of the population brought with it a need to focus on the misery of children.

Within this whole process of awakening to the child, however, curative education played a particular role; the following is an attempt to describe this role.

2. What is curative education?

When Professor H. Emminghaus published his book on the psychic disturbances of childhood in 1887 there were only very few studies about mental deficiencies in children he could refer to in the chapter on the history of child psychosis. There were a few articles about child psychology, observations on cretinism, epilepsy, and their connection with childhood disability. All these studies and approaches attempted to classify mental deficiencies in children; but the important thing was that all these approaches (which began around 1830) focused on the child and his special abnormalities. In his book *The Physiology and Pathology of the Mind*, published 1867, H. Maudsley (1835–1918) attempted the following classification of childhood disability and abnormal mental conditions:

I. Monomania and partial conceptual insanity
II. Chorea-like delirium
III. Cataleptic insanity which particularly manifests itself in the small child
IV. Epileptic insanity
V. Manic obsession
VI. Melancholy
VII. Affective and moral insanity

This classification is not mentioned here for its relevance but to show that already at that time there were enough observations of children available to make these classifications.

In 1866, just prior to the publication of Maudsley's book, the English doctor Langdon-Down wrote a booklet, *Observations on an Ethnic Classification of Idiots,* in which he tried to group the various forms of idiocy and imbecility according to racial characteristics. This also brings him to give a first description of what he called mongolism, which is now know after him as Down's syndrome.

For us, however, the following passage from Emminghaus' book is relevant:

> At the beginning of the [eighteen] fifties a separate department for mentally ill children (and adolescent individuals) was established at the Bicêtre in Paris. The medical director of this department was Paulmier who gained distinctive recognition through publishing statistical information about the incidence of childhood psychosis and through a clinical approach to manic obsessions in children and young people.

So, here a special department for mentally ill children was established; however, this led to statistical surveys and psychiatric studies.

At the time at this famous Hospital Bicêtre a doctor worked who could justifiably be called one of the founders of curative education. As long ago as 1843, Séguin published his work of two volumes, *Traitement moral, hygiène et education des idiots.* He wrote of his experiences since 1828 when a department for mentally ill children was opened at the Hospital Bicêtre by Séguin's teacher, Jean-Marc Itard (1775–1838).

Itard was actually an otologist, an ear specialist. He was the first to publish a textbook on otology *(Traité des maladies de l'oreille et de l'audition)* in 1821. He had also worked especially on the education of deaf children, when in 1798 the 'wild child of

Aveyron' was brought to him. Huntsmen had found a completely neglected, approximately ten-year-old child living on his
own in the forest in Aveyron in the south of France, and Itard
was asked how to deal with him. He took this child and tried,
with much love and enthusiasm, to educate him; he was successful in guiding this boy so that he became 'socially presentable,' but he could not teach him higher intellectual skills. He
summarized his experiences in a small publication. Through his
action, however, he laid the foundation for curative education.
Séguin became his student and not only established the first
home for disabled children in Massachusetts in 1846 together
with an American, Samuel Gridley Howe, but also tried to start
a real curative-educational movement.

A few years earlier, in 1836, the following happened. A young
medical student, Hans Jakob Guggenbühl (1816–63) was walking in the Swiss Alps, and in Seedorf in Canton Uri, he met a
girl suffering from cretinism who knelt in front of a picture of
the Virgin Mary and clearly spoke a Hail Mary.

> The sight moved me so deeply that I decided to
> completely dedicate myself to these miserable ones. A
> being capable of turning thoughts to God in this way is
> worthy of every attention and every sacrifice. Do these
> individuals of our species, these adulterated brothers, not
> deserve our interest much more than all the animals
> which people so busily try to breed to perfection?

This is what Guggenbühl himself writes about the experience. One of his biographers reports that Guggenbühl was so
deeply moved by this experience that he solemnly pledged to
'dedicate his life to finding a remedy for this misery and rather
die than abandon this issue of humanity.'

After this experience Guggenbühl intensely studied the
nature of cretinism, and in doing so he came across a publication
of the great physician and scientist P. V. Troxler with whom he
corresponded and whom he then met. In 1837 he qualified in

medicine at the University of Berne and in 1840 he published his appeal for help to fight cretinism. A year later, in 1841, he opened an institute for the education of people suffering from cretinism at Abendberg near Interlaken. Here Guggenbühl tried to develop a medical-educative therapy. He was utterly convinced that the high altitude, fresh drinking water, the special form of heating were the basic requirements for therapy. He devised special methods for teaching writing and numeracy, promoted the idea of building 'model villages' for the wellbeing of those suffering from cretinism, and his great enthusiasm soon led to institutes being built in Europe and America following his model. Yet he had his hands full with fighting off opposition from his fellow countrymen, and in 1863 he died of heart disease, just forty-seven years of age.

In his will the institute was given to the Herrnhuter brotherhood, but they refused the legacy and soon after the institute had to be closed. But the spirit of Guggenbühl's work and his immense dedication continue to live on in many curative-educational projects.

Itard, Séguin and Guggenbühl can be regarded as the three founders of curative education. But why, actually, these three? Why not Emminghaus or Maudsley? Itard's and Guggenbühl's biographies show particularly clearly what distinguishes them. The beginning of their curative-educational work is marked by a special experience.

Itard saw the 'wild boy of Aveyron,' Guggenbühl the praying girl suffering from cretinism. At that moment each of them resolved to help, in fact to help through their own immediate involvement, not just to study and to record, not only to examine and to diagnose, but 'to intend to do the good.'

This 'intending to do the good,' however, is often the starting point of an educational or social service. What is so special about Itard's and Guggenbühl's resolve? Both encountered a special type of 'human being.' The French doctor saw a human being degraded to an animal by neglect and loneliness. The Swiss medical student encountered in the praying girl a deformed human being who despite her deformity was capable of articulating the 'thoughts of God.' Both feel the need to bring the degenerated, the deformed image of the human being back to its eternal destiny. It is not just the impulse to cure an ill person, it is the intention of returning to its origin something that is detached.

In these two resolves to act I see the archetypical phenomenon of an awakening curative education. Because to me curative education does not seem to be a combination of curing and educating (as Strümpell said) but a completely new, third element. If sodium combines with chlorine to form salt then this substance is more than just the sum of the two others; in the same way curative education is something completely new, an impulse which did not exist in humanity before or not in such an obvious way. Curative education is the impulse to restore in other people the image of God if, due to circumstances or inner suffering and aberration, they do not represent this image any more. This means to develop in each person the ability to walk, to speak and to think through guidance and education because these three abilities are the expression of true humanity.

This impulse lived in Itard, in Séguin, in Guggenbühl. Where else can this impulse be found?

3. Where does the curative-educational impulse appear?

In a poor area I saw the misery of children who had been hired out by the communities to the farmers; I saw how virtually all of these children were — I could almost say — destroyed in body and soul by the oppressive cruelty of self-interest. Many of them, lacking courage in a lifeless, dire existence, can only develop a little strength for themselves and the homeland ...

It is a matter of personal experience that very soon
they rise from the deep misery of deprivation towards a
sense of humanity, trust and friendship — the experience
that humanity uplifts the soul even of the most deprived
person, that the eyes of a poor, abandoned child shines
with emotional amazement if after years of hardship a
gentle human hand offers to guide him.

These words were written by Heinrich Pestalozzi on December 9, 1775 in his *Appeal to Philanthropists and Benefactors to the Kind Support of an Institute in a Country House for Providing Poor Children with Education and Work*. With these words the initial impulse of curative education came into being. Although the project in the Neuhaus failed, the impulse lived on.

Reporting his experiences in Stans to a friend, Pestalozzi wrote:

Most children were, on arrival, in a condition which is
the consequence of the utmost degradation of general
human nature. Many came with deeply ingrown scabies
so that they were hardly able to walk, many with broken
skin on their heads, many in rags which were infested
with bugs, many gaunt, like wasted skeletons, yellow,
grinning, with eyes full of fear and brows furrowed with
mistrust and concern, some full of bold impudence, used
to begging, faking and all crookedness; others oppressed
by the misery, passive but mistrusting, without love and
full of fear.

Here everything is already described that was later the general misery of children across the whole of Europe. These children were in this state of neglect because the armies of the French Revolution marched across Switzerland. (Remarkable how in Pestalozzi there is an ever-recurring motive: his inner connection to the French Revolution and his immense power as a curative educator.

Already after a few weeks he had transformed these children in Stans into real human beings. How did this happen? In the same letter he says:

> From morning to night I was as good as on my own with them. Everything good that happened to them in body and soul came from my hand. Every support, every helping hand offered when in trouble, every lesson they received directly from me. My hand held their hand, my eyes looked into their eyes. I shed tears when they cried and my smile accompanied theirs. They were out of the world, they were out of Stans, they were with me and I was with them. Their soup was mine, their drink was mine.

These words sound like a gospel of curative education, and they are written in 1799, the same year as in Itard the intention of curative education arose. In that same year Napoleon abandoned his campaign in Egypt and seized power in Paris on November 9. He became first consul and consequently the absolute sovereign of France. The orphans of Stans, however, and their father, the curative educator Pestalozzi, were again driven into misery and poverty.

Twice thirty-three years later, in December 1866, in the same year as Dr Langdon-Down wrote his study on the classification of retarded children and coined the term 'mongolism,' a conversation took place in London, in the slums of the eastern part of the city. Again it was a young twenty-one-year-old medical student and a small ten-year-old boy. The evening class which the young medical student had held in a dilapidated wooden house for the poor people of the district had finished and everybody apart from the little boy, Jim Jarvis, had left. Now the student wanted to send Jim away, too, but Jim asked him if he could stay overnight, as he had neither father nor mother, nor any home at all. Consequently, the student, Thomas John Barnardo, took him to his place, gave him something to eat and at midnight, it was in the middle of December, he set off together with Jim. Where to? Jim had told him that not just he but many hundreds of children in London were forced to spend their nights outside. Barnardo, who had already been living for four years among the poorest of the poor, first in Dublin and then in London, belonged to the 'Awakened' and he did not want to believe Jim. But in this night he saw a number of children sleeping on the roof of a shed, all in ragged clothes, without blankets, in the grey cold of the big city.

Barnardo had wanted to become a missionary in China, but he now found that his China was here in London and that he needed to help these neglected, abandoned, orphaned children. He founded the East End Juvenile Mission. In March 1868 he opened his first home in London. Barnardo's work progressed with amazing speed. Home after home was opened, many homeless children found accommodation and education, and then on February 14, 1873 a big hall which formerly had served as a gin palace opened, Lord Shaftesbury held a speech along the following lines:

> Without doubt the churches of today do good work; but they are lacking initiative; they seem to think that it is enough to open a building and to announce that religion is for sale there. But this cannot be enough to bring the majority back to the faith; you have to follow the word of the Gospel which says, 'Go quickly into the streets and alleys of the city and invite the poor, the crippled, the lame and the blind,' and, 'Go out into the country lanes and behind the hedges and urge anyone you can find to come, so that my house will be full.'

You could not have found a more accurate description for what inspired Dr Barnardo. He did his work in the spirit of the biblical wedding feast. He looked for the poor and the lame, the abandoned and homeless and tried to transform them back into human beings.

When he died on September 19, 1905 he had been father, teacher and example for some sixty thousand children whom he had given a life in decent conditions in small homes and village-like communities. His will began with words along the following lines: 'Death and the grave are passing bonds ... I hope to die in the same way as I have lived; in the humble yet steadfast belief in Jesus Christ whom I tried to serve in such an inadequate way.'

In the year of Dr Barnardo's death — he like Guggenbühl, died of heart disease — the Viennese author, Jakob Wassermann, was struggling to write a book which he began and abandoned over and over again until he had found the right tone and the right title, *Caspar Hauser: The Inertia of the Heart.** The book has the following dedication:

> Still to our eyes the self-same sun
> Smiles on the self-same earth!
> Out of the self-same blood and slime
> God, man and child have birth!
> Naught remains, but naught is lost:
> That which is old was young,
> And that which is young was old:
> Life and death are bound together
> And the Symbol is the Form.

In 1841 (in the same year when Jakob Guggenbühl founded his institute at Abendberg) a young Italian completed his theological studies and was ordained to the Catholic priesthood in Turin. He was exactly one year older than Guggenbühl and the child of poor peasants in the Piedmont. His father died when he was two years old and from early childhood onwards he had to work hard on his mother's farm. There was no opportunity to attend school. At the age of eleven he went away and became a farm labourer. He herded goats and worked in a dairy to

---

* The English translation was published under the title, *Caspar Hauser, Enigma of a Century.*

eventually be able to attend the Latin school. At the same time he worked for a tailor for his living and later for a confectioner. In this way he made it through school and the seminary until he was ordained.

Then his real work began which he had been longing for the whole time. He gathered all the neglected boys from Turin, the beggars and thieves, the scallywags and idlers. Every Sunday he took them out of the city of Turin, gave them some lessons, but mainly just played with them. He was better at running and jumping, laughing and chasing than all of them put together. He became their acknowledged leader and protector. Within a year he had gathered two hundred of them, and it was not his strictness but his strength and kindness, his courage and his passion that kept this gang together.

Within two years there were seven hundred boys, newsboys, errand boys, cart-boys and vagabonds. He was as much frowned upon as they were. 'What business has a priest with this rabble?' The episcopal authorities brought a case against this priest on the grounds of insanity, but Giovanni Bosco's cleverness saved him.

He then tried to purchase a permanent home for his boys. At last, after much effort he was successful and was able to set up a real school for his pupils and, even better, training workshops; this took place in 1853. After he created schools and training workshops he started to build a church, opened a secondary school for financially disadvantaged students and trained teachers. He founded the Salesian Order which, at his death in 1888, was represented all over Europe and South America. Today [1950] the order has 12 000 members and manages many hundreds of schools and workplaces.

Don Bosco was convinced that every young person was good at heart. Only if social circumstances suppress what is good, will it not be able to develop. In his schools hitting a child was forbidden; punishing or suppressing a child was forbidden. Prevention, not punishment was Don Bosco's educational programme. Teachers had to be an example for their pupils and had to develop the pupils' trust and love for what is good. For hundreds of thousands of young people Don Bosco became a father; he, who achieved real miracles with them, guided them to true humanity. Many years later the Catholic Church felt the need to make him a saint.

The revolutionary Pestalozzi, the Methodist Barnardo, the Catholic priest Don Bosco — in the centre, in the north and in the south of Europe the impulse of curative education awoke through them, lived through them and grew. They were not 'official' representatives of curative education, rather the true practitioners.

But what was the course of formal curative education?

4. The course of curative education

Apart from these three pioneers,

> Heinrich Pestalozzi (1746–1827)
> Giovanni Bosco (1815–88)
> John Thomas Barnardo (1845–1905)

who carry the curative-educational impulse, the intention to save the eternal image of the human being in the social conditions of their time and put it into practice, there are the actual founders of curative education:

> Jean-Marc Gaspard Itard (1775–1838)
> Emanuel Séguin (1790–1869)
> Hans Jakob Guggenbühl (1816–1863).

These three truly gave their support and attention to so-called disabled people and to those with behavioural problems.

Apart from those there were many others who felt the same impulse at the same time. For example, as early as 1816 Gerhard Guggenmoos, a teacher, founded an institute in Salzburg for the deaf and those suffering from cretinism. Karl Friedrich Kern, a doctor, founded a model educational institute for children with behavioural problems in Mockern, Thuringia, in 1853. Katenkamp, a farmer, followed an inner impulse, studied education, became a teacher for deaf-mute children and established a private institute in Dehnenhorst in 1845. Then there were Protestant ministers and Catholic priests who became aware of the curative-educational task. As a result charitable institutes were created like the one in Wildberg, Württemberg, in 1835, the institute in Stetten, Württemberg, in 1848, Eckberg 1854, Nuremberg 1854, the Alsterdorfer Institute in 1867 and Bethel near Bielefeld in 1872.

The beginning of each of these foundations is marked by the enthusiasm and dedication of individuals. The intention 'to do good' prompted men like Probst, Sengelmann, Bodelschwingh to take action. During these founding years of the curative-educational movement the main concern of each of these men and women was the divine origin of human existence.

It is astonishing to see how many of these institutes were concerned with the education and instruction of deaf-mute children. Historically the education of deaf-mute children is the mother soil of curative education.

It actually developed from efforts to teach deaf-mute children to read and write, to speak and to express themselves. These efforts date back to the sixteenth century (Pedro de Ponce), were then taken up by the Swiss doctor Aman (1669–1742) who lived in Holland, and were continued by the two great teachers who worked in the education of deaf-mute children, the French priest Charles Michel de l'Epée (1712–89) and Samuel Heinicke (1727–90) from the north of Germany. Both worked during the same period; the Frenchman particularly supported sign language as a measure of educating deaf-mute children whereas the German man put his emphasis on the spoken language.

Although their achievements were extraordinary it is not yet sufficiently appreciated that both had the same aspiration despite the fact that their methods were in opposition. 'The child is deaf and mute; how can I help this child to assert himself as a person despite this evil?' However, it would have been a different, more curative-educational question if these two pioneers had asked themselves, 'How can we overcome the deafness as such? How can we make the deaf child hear again?'

Here I see a historical symptom which needs to be reflected clearly in order to understand the history of curative education. Eighteenth century rationalism increasingly saw the human being as fallen from the divine. He comes into the world burdened with weaknesses, deformities and ills, and humanitarian yet rational efforts are needed to help him as much as possible. Heinicke as well as de l'Epée are children of this rationalism. Only at the turn of the century was the human mind captured by a new 'affinity to God.' Whether they are English romantic poets like Shelley, Wordsworth and Keats, or the great German philosophers Schelling, Hegel and Fichte, or the romantic poets Novalis, Arnim, Tieck and Brentano, or whether the romantic scientists Troxler and Oken or Itard and Guggenbühl — in all of them there was something new, something totally unprecedented.

We need to ask ourselves why this happened at that particular historic moment at the turn of the eighteenth to the nineteenth century. It was the time when Goethe wrote his *Wilhelm Meister* — his *Bildungsroman,* an educational novel where Mignon, a disabled girl, is the central character — and Schiller drafted his *Letters on the Aesthetic Education of Man.* Everywhere, in England, Germany, Russia, Poland and Italy people began to turn again to spirituality. People like Pestalozzi and Lavater, Oberlin and Jung-Stilling tried to work quietly in the background.

This is the era of Napoleon when a single man attempted to conquer the world, when people were used as pawns, warfare was sparked as a mass craze and the dignity of the individual human being was spurned. At this special moment in history curative education as an impulse was born in Itard and Pestalozzi. Guggenbühl and Séguin took it up, Don Bosco and

Barnardo took it further, although both Don Bosco and Barnardo left the field of curative education to enter the social field of corrective training. Why did this happen?

Because from about 1835 onwards the materialism of the nineteenth century developed. Physiology and neurology, psychiatry and surgery, physics and chemistry began to hold their ground. Romantic idealism and classic Goetheanism were hidden behind the looming clouds of materialistic atheism. In the year 1850 experimental psychology began with Fechner, Wundt, and Helmholtz. Hypnosis treatment, which dissociated itself from mesmerism, was introduced in the developing field of psychiatry. The brain and the spinal chord were more and more regarded as reflex centres and the whole of the neural functions was studied as a reflex apparatus. Mental illnesses were interpreted as brain diseases and the characteristics of the human soul were assessed as the result of neural functioning.

Then, at the dawn of the twentieth century, genetics and psychoanalysis were first mentioned. The subsurface of human existence was explored and its understanding, based on evolutionary theory, took its starting point in the animal. What could possibly be left for the child with behavioural problems, for the neurotic and psychopathic, for the lame and epileptic child?

At the beginning of the twentieth century intelligence assessment was introduced. Every child was to be subjected to an intelligence test in order to assess his abilities and potential. But in the meantime everywhere, particularly in Germany and Switzerland, schools for children with learning difficulties were founded. What does that mean?

Let us look back once more. At the turn of the eighteenth to the nineteenth century individuals and groups of people were attracted by a movement of spiritual solidarity. As a result the Napoleonic despotism was counterbalanced, and it was not Napoleon's intentions, but the tendencies of humanity that won the day.

In opposition to this the powers of rising materialism gathered and stifled romantic and Goetheanistic spiritual under-standing. Curative education, sprouting on the ground of educa-tion of deaf-mutes, flourished briefly only to die down again.

In his book on the psychopathology of childhood, Hom-burger wrote about this first appearance of curative education:

> This first period of foundations by teachers shows quite clearly that even great talent, acknowledged success and lofty idealism do not continue working beyond the lives of the leaders if they lack in economic understanding, if they are not practical people, if state and church (the public education authorities) respond with lack of understanding or opposition. Once the initial educa-tional enthusiasm had run out of steam the teacher was merely a poor school master who was looked down on, and who had no say in public life.[1]

This describes the curative-educational situation at the middle of the nineteenth century. Curative-educational enthusi-asm had run out of steam but, in truth, not because these first pioneers were not 'practical people' but because there were three powerful opponents to this small number of curative educators: church, state and science.

The church, for good as well as bad reasons, opposed curative educators until eventually some institutes became either fully Catholic or fully Protestant. These homes and institutes were filled with an air of mission and care. This, however, kills cura-tive education as an impulse. It is charity which prevails.

In science, psychiatry and neurology claimed curative educa-tion as their domain of research and from the 1860s onwards required curative-educational institutes to be under the control of psychiatrists.

The state, through increasing nationalization of education and welfare services, made its claims. Kern and Stötzner demanded national schools for children with learning difficulties to be cre-ated in 1863. In the course of the following decades public welfare services became more and more nationalized and centralized. At first special classes were created and then, in several cities, complete special schools (Dresden in 1867, Elberfeld in 1879, Leipzig in 1881, Dortmund in 1883, Aachen, Düsseldorf, Kassel, Lübeck in 1888, Bremen, Altona, Frankfurt and others in 1889.)

Through this, however, the actual, true curative-educational impulse had been killed off. To avoid misunderstandings, I do not mean that the charitable institutes of the church, the national schools for children with learning difficulties, the curative-educational departments of the institutes for mentally ill people did not achieve anything good. Many dedicated people worked there, helped and nursed, hoped, researched and studied. Many thousands of pupils with special needs were supported and educated; but curative education as such was defeated by this threefold campaign. These special, selected, stigmatized children became the prey of the three great powers arising from the materialism of the time. But where does the source of true curative education spring up again?

This section cannot be concluded without remembering a person who, like a transfiguration on a mountain, appeared in order to shine — as a sign and symptom — over the first awakening of curative education.

On Whit Monday of the year 1828 all of a sudden, as if conjured from the air, a young person appeared in Nuremberg. He was hardly able to speak, he looked quite miserable, and his feet which were stuck in heavy boots were covered with blood. Nobody, even he himself, knew where he came from. He just happened to be there. At first the police put him in jail but then he was handed over to Friedrich Daumer for education.

Anselm von Feuerbach, an upright and famous man, adopted him and wrote a book about him in which he described the extraordinary destiny and special characteristics of Kaspar Hauser and traced back his origin to the court in Baden and thus to the realm of Napoleon.

Several times Kaspar Hauser was assaulted by unidentified

attackers and was finally stabbed in the heart in Ansbach palace gardens on December 14, 1833. On December, 17 he died of his wounds. The inscription on his gravestone reads:

HIC JACET
CASPARUS HAUSER
AENIGMA
SUI TEMPORIS
IGNOTA NATIVITATIS
OCCULTA MORS★

A young person unable to adjust to life on earth, of obscure origin, poor, at first only able to take water and bread but able to calm animals and waken what is good in the people he encountered, received an education, adjusted to life around him, and died at the hands of murderers.

Life and death are bound together
And the Symbol is the Form[2]

Does not each of the so-called difficult to educate, retarded children come into life in a way similar to Kaspar Hauser? Poor, strange, an enigma and yet a blessing where they are met with an open heart? This 'Child of Europe,' as Kaspar Hauser was soon called, marked the beginning of curative education in the same way as the 'wild boy of Aveyron.'

The debate about Kaspar Hauser, his origin and destiny, continues to this day. The representatives of church, state and science fought him in the same way as they tried to suppress curative education; his origin and destiny were covered up by the blue coat of the charity, the grey cloth of the state, and the black veil of science. Despite this the memory of this human being lives on in the hearts of those who still try to fight against the 'crime against the human soul.'

★ Here lies / Caspar Hauser / enigma / of his time / unknown birth / mysterious death

Although Napoleon was defeated in 1812 and 1813 and then imprisoned, his impulse to war and tyranny prevailed through the course of the nineteenth century. Technology spread across the world, proletarization of humankind was brought about, and materialism took hold of the soul.

Together with Kaspar Hauser, with Goetheanism and romantic idealism, true curative education had to retreat into the catacombs.

But the springs did not run dry; they only needed to be rediscovered and opened and this happened in the following way.

5. Rudolf Steiner's advice is sought

In 1923 there were two young curative educators working in one of the few curative-educational institutes which had been founded on private initiative. Franz Löffler and Siegfried Pickert's course of destiny had brought them into contact with Rudolf Steiner's anthroposophy. Franz Löffler recalls:

> We were following our vocation but were unable to reconcile this vocation with what was living in us through anthroposophy. Our aspiration for an understanding of the human being and the world had to be pursued outside our work ... Living closely together with children who were mentally ill required daily decisions which we were unable to take guided solely by the personal relationship with the children, but guided from an understanding of the illness as such. Here we experienced a rift. How could we facilitate healing? This question was deep in our soul while living and working for twelve to fourteen hours every day with these children in need of soul care.[3]

With this question (which arose, note well, from the teachers, not the doctors) these two young people, together with a third, Albrecht Strohschein, approached Rudolf Steiner. This encounter took place at Christmas 1923. Pickert wrote about this:

> In a personal conversation we were able to tell Rudolf
> Steiner about our work and to put forward our questions
> ... Then answers were given for everything that was
> asked and much that was unspoken but living within us
> ... He talked about how so-called 'abnormal' children
> with their 'I' and their astral body are only incompletely
> incarnated and are already, especially when asleep,
> preparing the embodiment of a future life on earth; how
> the curative educator needs to keep this in mind and can
> practice as an imaginative exercise what these children
> have not achieved in their present incarnation.
>
> Rudolf Steiner said: 'When I visit the class for
> children with learning difficulties in Stuttgart I tell
> myself that here work is done for a future life on earth,
> quite apart from what is achieved now, and that can be
> quite a lot ... According to my research nearly every
> genius has gone through such a poor existence in a
> former life on earth.' And in a few sentences there was
> an abundance of practical advice for speech formation
> therapy, eurythmy, writing, reading, motor skill exercises
> and medical help, all of which were interventions aiming
> to deliberately and lovingly make the real spirituality take
> hold of the body.[4]

Reading these words I feel that at this moment the springs of curative education began to flow again. Because from now on the nature of these children was newly opened up, guided by spiritual understanding. The knowledge of repeated lives on earth, of karma and reincarnation, was given to curative educators to help them with their task.

Rudolf Steiner gave this brief conversation very serious consideration. Soon afterwards the three young people found a house in Jena, the Lauenstein, which, without any funds and solely on the strength of being resolved 'to do the good,' they transformed into a 'home for children in need of soul care' (a name suggested by Rudolf Steiner). Rudolf Steiner visited this house on June 18, 1924, gave advice and instructions and then held the Curative Education Course from June 25 to July 7. In twelve lectures he provided the anthroposophical foundations of curative education. He described the types of children in need of soul care on the strength of a detailed knowledge which was astonishing and moving. He supplied information about the physical-emotional-intellectual patterns of these children and gave detailed advice regarding therapy and practical curative-educational work.

Yet this course contains more. In almost every lecture it addresses the curative educator's inner attitude towards the child, and by this Rudolf Steiner opened up the possibility that a continuous curative-educational course of action can develop from an immediate understanding of the curative-educational situation, and not from lifeless academic theory. The curative educator needs to become an artist whose actions are guided by spiritual knowledge. So in his tenth lecture, Rudolf Steiner appealed to the future curative educators:

> Can't you become dancers? [An appeal in the sense of
> Nietzsche's *Zarathustra*] You should be leading lives of
> joy — deep inner joy in the truth! There is nothing in
> the world more delightful, nothing more fascinating than
> the experience of truth.[5]

These lectures contain a whole 'catechism for future curative educators' and combine spiritual understanding, curative-educational practice and medical work in a comprehensive concept of the coming curative education.

The various conditions of children and young people in need of soul care were studied from a completely different perspective. For example, the types of seizures which are summarized as epilepsy were classified in two major groups: those which are not accompanied by moral abnormalities and those with moral abnormalities. Each of these groups was described in detail and the interventions required for healing identified.

The field of childhood hysteria was described as an overly intense process of incarnation and therefore is made conceptually accessible for the first time. Thus epilepsy is seen as an event associated with birth, and hysteria as a process tending towards death.

Rudolf Steiner spoke in detail about the phenomena of obsessive ideas and compulsive acts; he covered the field of cleptomania and gradual mental enfeeblement. He provided information about the big issues of laterality, albinism and childhood neurosis. And underlying all of his presentations was a profound understanding of the human being which facilitates the immediate deduction of the appropriate therapeutical intervention from accurate diagnosis.

Here ecclesiastical charity is replaced with an empathic love which recognizes the higher human being in every person in need of soul care. Medical-psychological-psychiatric expertise is replaced with healing guided by an understanding of the human being as a microcosm within the macrocosm. The curative educator's engagement within the framework of public employment, however, is replaced by the curative educator's self-education carried out as part of his daily experience.

After this course Rudolf Steiner integrated curative education within the framework of the Medical Section of the School of Spiritual Science and placing it with Dr Ita Wegman, at the time the head of that Section. She was a consistent and faithful supporter of curative education. She saw the cultural effects and the social purposes of this work and probably contributed most to its growth.

It is due to Ita Wegman's work that today there are many curative-educational institutes in Switzerland and Germany, England and Scotland, in Sweden and Iceland, founded on private initiative, which aim to enliven curative education through anthroposophy. In these institutes about a thousand children in need of soul care are cared for and educated.

Three times thirty-three years after his first appearance, the being of Kaspar Hauser, who was doomed by the inertia of the hearts of those around him, is resurrected in Rudolf Steiner's curative-educational course.

Since this course, it is no longer a disgrace to be born as a cripple or idiot, as a simpleton or epileptic. Because in every one of these people there is a spirit-soul as in everyone else; there are no social distinctions but just stages of the capacity to incarnation which vary from person to person.

What Lessing had once dimly grasped, and thus falteringly expressed in his book, *The Education of the Human Race*, can now become true heart-knowledge. The last three paragraphs of his book may conclude this section.

> Why should I not come back as often as I am capable of acquiring fresh knowledge, fresh expertness? Do I bring away so much from once, that there is nothing to repay the trouble of coming back?
>
> Is this a reason against it? Or, because I forget that I have been here already? Happy is it for me that I do forget. The recollection of my former condition would permit me to make only a bad use of the present. And that which even I must forget now, is that necessarily forgotten for ever?
>
> Or is it a reason against the hypothesis that so much time would have been lost to me? Lost — and how much then should I miss? — Is not a whole Eternity mine?

6. Epilogue

Many people keep wondering why Goethe allocated such a major role to the figure of Mignon in *Wilhelm Meister's Apprenticeship,* why he even once described Mignon as the actual hero of this novel.

The writing of the *Apprenticeship* happened during an important period in Goethe's life. He started the book in April 1794 and finished it on June 26, 1796. This completed the total reworking of *Wilhelm Meister's Theatrical Mission.* At this time in July 1794, however, Goethe met Schiller, marking the beginning of their friendship. The *Fairy Tale* was also written during these determining years of Goethe's life while the character of Mignon was vividly on his mind.

Mignon is a child in need of soul care. Through birth and circumstances she has become a riddle of the soul for everyone who has met her. Despite being full of love and dedication, this person is still unable to assert herself in life. However, the way Goethe introduced this figure in his novel, how he developed her through it, let her die and be buried, the way the Marquis, at her marble coffin, recognized her as his niece and revealed her past to the Abbé, shows that Goethe was one of the first people in the West who tried to unveil the mystery of reincarnation and karma.

As Gretchen is for Faust, Mignon is for Wilhelm the eternal feminine figure who leads and protects him in spiritual worlds. Although she is a poor, strange, retarded child she is an eternal being in the spiritual sphere. At her coffin the Abbé says:

> Of the child whom we are burying now we have but
> little to say. We do not even yet know whence she came;
> we are not acquainted with her parents, and can only
> guess at the number of her years. Her deep, reserved

heart, scarcely allowed us to conjecture its inmost
secrets; nothing in her was clear, nothing manifest, but
her love to the man who had saved her from the hands
of a barbarian.

Thirty-three years after Goethe had written these words
Kaspar Hauser appeared in Nuremberg. About him, too,
people had little to say; they did not know whence he came,
and his deep, reserved heart scarcely allowed conjecture about
its inmost secrets. He also showed deep love for those who
again and again tried to help him; Anselm von Feuerbach, who
genuinely tried, and Lord Stanhope, who pretended to
do so.

But what Goethe really thought and felt about Mignon he
once told Müller, the provost, in a conversation: the whole work
had been written because of this particular character. This also
becomes evident at the point when Mignon dresses in women's
clothes for the first time. When she, clothed in an angel's robe,
steps into the circle of her playmates the following conversation
develops:

> 'Are you an angel?' said one child.
> 'I wish I were,' answered Mignon.
> 'Why are you holding a lily?'
> 'My heart ought to be as pure and open; then I should
> be happy.'
> 'Where are your wings — let us see them.'
> 'They represent more beautiful ones, which are not
> yet unfolded.'

Here Mignon talks about her imminent death and about how
all that cannot come about during her present life will happen
after she has died. For this reason this child seems like an archetype of all children in need of soul care. Whoever is really close
to them and working with them needs to know about their
higher being, and only this will give the strength and enlighten-

ment necessary to carry out here and now what will be accomplished at a later stage.

For this reason Rudolf Steiner also said in the second lecture of the Curative Education course:

> For it is indeed true, and we must be conscious of the
> fact: in educating handicapped children we are
> intervening in a process which in the normal course of
> development — were there no intervention, or were
> there misguided intervention — would find its
> fulfilment only when the child had passed through the
> gate of death and come to birth again in the next life. We
> are making, that is to say, a deep intervention in karma.
> Whenever we give treatment to a handicapped child, we
> are *intervening in karma*.[6]

Schiller was deeply moved by the character of Mignon, and on July 1, 1796 wrote to Goethe:

> Everything you do with Mignon, whether alive or
> dead, is extraordinarily beautiful. Her isolated character,
> her mysterious existence, her purity and innocence
> represent the stage of life where she is, so pure, it can
> move one to the purest wistfulness and to a truly human
> sadness because in her nothing but pure humanity is
> represented.

That in Mignon 'nothing but pure humanity' is represented is the moving experience conveyed by this figure. With her, who in Goethe's mind developed as the central character of the Wilhelm Meister novel, the archetype of the child in need of soul care is born at the same time. In this sphere, too, Goethe had anticipated a new spiritual understanding. He had recognized the character of the retarded child in its truth.

For this reason, when asked to take off the angel's robe, Mignon refuses and sings the immortal verses:

Such let me seem till such I be;
Take not my snow-white dress away!
Soon from this dusk of earth I flee
Up to the glittering lands of day.

There first a little time I rest,
Then wake so glad, to scene so kind;
In earthly robes no longer dress'd,
This band, this girdle left behind.

And those calm shining sons of morn
They ask not who is maid or boy;
No robes, no garments there are worn,
Our body pure from sin's alloy.

Through little life not much I toil'd,
Yet anguish long this heart has wrung,
Untimely woe my blossom spoil'd;
Make me again forever young!

This sigh: 'Make me again forever young!' is expressed by
each child in need of soul care. Listening to it is the task of curative education. Its aim here on earth is to help form the trans-
figured body in every human being so that the good can prevail.

10

Adalbert Stifter and
Curative Education

1

At the beginning of the nineteenth century, with the awakening of a new insight into the nature of the human being, a new tone was set in the hearts of many people. What seemed to have been lying in darkness for centuries, what, since Paracelsus' days, had ceased to reveal itself in the light of thought, reappeared now in diverse form. Then the intellectual need to be able to see again the true image of the human being was roused. This was the new tone which resounded in the consciences of many people. At the same time events occurred almost everywhere in Europe which emerged from this need.

Goethe created, as some kind of first call, the character of Mignon, in whom he tried to awaken the concealed spiritual form of the human being. Professor Itard took the 'wild boy of Aveyron' into his home to educate him to become a human being; Pestalozzi attempted to found his institutes in Neuhaus and Stans. Johannes Falk, after having lost his own children to an epidemic, was led by dreams and visions to open an Institute for Neglected Boys which set the initial impulse for the Rauhe Haus. Compassion for all creatures was a trait of the time and it appealed to people's hearts like a new beginning.

In line with this were phenomena like the visions of

Katharina von Emmerich, the appearance of Frau von Krüderer and her remarkable travels through Europe, Jung-Stilling's inner visions, Friedrich Oberlin's work in Alsace, Brentano's conversion through Katharina von Emmerich, Justinus Kerner's contact with the seer of Prevost, the young Mörike's encounter with the strange character Peregrina, and Friedrich Schlegel's religious conversion. Yet Hölderlin's mental derangement, Schelling's temporary silence, Caroline's sudden death and other events which corresponded to the spirit of this era were also part of the picture.

A first dawn appeared at the spiritual horizon of an awakening era which was full of anticipation of the true nature of the human being. Into this spiritual atmosphere Adalbert Stifter was born. Even though his birth place took place far away from these events a hint of what was happening still imbued itself on his developing soul. His year of birth, 1805, is in the midst of this search for a new image of the human being.

Stifter was born at the source of the Vltava, and this river gave his soul another foundation. The Vltava is the heart of the Bohemian landscape, and its tragic beauty was absorbed by the child's mind. It provided him with the trait of noble resignation and the wish to become an educator fostering morality, laws, and integrity and opposing everything compulsive, excessive, and tyrannical. The same landscape had a part in forming and educating the noble-minded Amos Comenius, providing him with the same foundation.

As a young man Stifter associated himself with a third element which he encountered at the educational institute Kremsmünster in Upper Austria. In this huge Benedictine monastery he experienced the spiritual oneness and learning of liberal Catholicism. There he was educated according to an old European tradition.

The following three powerful spiritual influences had a formative impact on Stifter's soul: the German anticipation of a new era which aspires to a new image of humanity; the Bohemian landscape with its calm yet resigned beauty; and the Austrian liberal Catholicism which had developed into a medium for true humanitarianism in those days.

These were the three factors which formed Stifter, and when as a twenty-one-year-old, he went to the university in Vienna in 1826, his personality was shaped. His individuality had found its appropriate form and now strived to meet its destiny. Like many of his young contemporaries he became a tutor in a number of aristocratic Viennese families, and his students loved and adored him. At this time he must have been a very spirited and attentive educator because he was much in demand, and for nearly twenty years, as a kind of perpetual student, he made his living from this tutoring.

During this period his inclination to become a painter gradually receded and was replaced by the wish to become a poet. This was a sacrifice, but this particular kind of sacrifice inspired the treasure of his narratives. Each of his works contains a portion of the three elements which formed Stifter. They aspire to a spiritual image of the human being; they describe nature and a landscape in calm resignation; they steadfastly maintain the tradition of morality and laws.

These are three elements which, transformed, are the foundation of all true educational work. For this reason especially the *Studies*, created in the years 1840 to 1850, are such eminently educational works. They educate the human being and help him to come closer to his highest destiny. I do not mean to say that these stories are reserved for the more mature young people, but that they are of educational value for everyone as long as they have an open heart. They help one to educate oneself.

2

At the time when Stifter experienced the content of the *Studies* welling up within him, shorter narratives also took shape which seemingly were not associated with a particular topic. Yet they are about child development and growth in relation to the environment.

Not until 1853 were these pieces, previously published individually, compiled in a book and published under the title *Bunte Steine* (Coloured Stones). Stifter's initial idea had been to publish these stories as a children's book, so the first title was Stories for Children, then Stories for Young People, until the poet realized that this was a book which is of concern to everyone.

The six individual parts in the book are called Granite, Limestone, Tourmaline, Rock Crystal, Fool's Gold and Bergmilch. The last story has been included as a kind of appendix and does not really belong to this series. A preface as well as an introduction was added to the book. In the now famous preface Stifter addresses his critics and in an emotionally touching way exposes the crystal which forms the inner principle of his poetry and aspiration. The fact that these statements introduce *Bunte Steine* shows the importance he attached to this little book. It starts with the following words:

> It was once remarked in criticism of me that I only
> imagine small things and that my people are always
> ordinary people. If that is true, then today I am in a
> position to offer my readers something still smaller and
> less significant, namely a variety of entertainments for
> young hearts. Not even virtue and morality are preached
> in them, as is customary, but they are to have their effect
> solely through what they are. If there is something noble
> and good in me, then it will repose in my writings.

And he continued by saying:

> But since we are talking of the great and the small, I shall
> set forth my views, which probably diverge from those
> of many other people. The flow of the air, the rippling of
> the water, the growth of the grain, the waves of the sea,

> the greening of the earth, the gleaming of the sky, the
> twinkling of the stars, I consider great ... As it is in outer
> nature, so it is in the inner nature of the human race. A
> whole life full of justice, simplicity, mastering oneself,
> reasonableness, effectiveness in one's circle, admiration
> of the beautiful, combined with cheerful, tranquil effort,
> I consider great; mighty movements of temperament,
> frightful outbursts of anger, the lust of vengeance, the
> inflamed spirit that strives for activity, tears down,
> destroys, and in its excitement often throws away its own
> life, I consider not greater, but smaller, for these things
> are as much products of individual and one-sided forces
> as storms, fire-spewing mountains, and earthquakes. We
> want to try to observe the *gentle* law that guides the
> human race.

Yet for Stifter the explanation of the 'gentle law' is associated
with a further element; in his view it is the basic condition for
the appropriate way of respecting and understanding the dignity
of the human being. His concern is the appreciation of the individual human being in his individuality and personality. In
whichever way the personality may appear, it needs to be
regarded as the sacred seal of the world spirit and each insult that
may be inflicted on it requires help and healing. The preface
continues:

> There are forces that aim for the survival of the
> individual. They take and use everything necessary to its
> survival and development. They secure the endurance of
> the one and thus of all. But if someone unreservedly
> seizes upon everything that his being needs, when he
> destroys the conditions for the existence of someone
> else, then something higher grows angry in us; we help
> the weak and oppressed; we restore the state of affairs in
> which one person can survive beside the other and walk

his human path; and when we have done that, we feel satisfied, we feel ourselves higher and more ardent than we feel as individuals, we feel ourselves as all humanity.

The voice of Pestalozzi resounds in these words; here are words for the longing which, at the start of the nineteenth century, aimed to reach hearts. The voice of mercy for the degraded and insulted image of the human being which, however concealed and distorted it may be, still has its own eternal existence and dignity. And Stifter adds:

> Thus there are forces at work toward the survival of mankind as a whole that may not be checked by individual forces, but on the contrary, they check the individual forces. It is the law of these forces, the law that wants everyone to be respected, honoured, and not be threatened alongside the other, that he may walk his higher human path, may earn the love and admiration of his fellow men, that he may be protected as a precious object, as every person is a precious object for all other persons.

Here the core of all curative education is put into words: that every person, regardless of what he is like, shall become a precious object for all others; that he, as an eternal human being, may not lose his worthiness, however strange his actions and behaviour may be.

In the *Bunte Steine* Stifter reflects on these forces which are 'at work toward the survival of mankind as a whole.' He wants to demonstrate which traits need to be acquired so that these forces can take their effect in the human being. These inconspicuous little stories contain precious contributions to acquiring a truly curative-educational morality. Because these contributions are based on reality they are pragmatic at the same time, that is, they are applicable to daily contact with the aberrations of the image of the human being.

I do not know whether Stifter was guided by deliberate insight when he selected and named these particular stories. I do not think, as most of Stifter's commentators do, that the naming after stones is arbitrary. A deeper insight shows a deeper meaning of these titles. Because how else would you name discipline and order which has substantiated itself through spiritual aspiration if not after stones? Moderation and morality, if acquired through inner practice, remains in the soul as a precious crystal and as a moulded form.

They are the virtues of the true curative educator, who does not simply wish to help out of disposition, but who intends to become a helper for lost individuals through the strength of acquired ability. Which of these traits Stifter had in mind will be explored by studying the five stories closer.

3

The first story, 'Granite,' was published under the title 'The Pitch Burner,' in 1849. It starts with Stifter's reminiscent description of an episode that took place in his early childhood. Once, when he was sitting in front of his parents' house, a passing hawker selling cart grease jokingly rubbed his feet with the dark resinous grease. He was so proud that he went straight into the house to show off his new acquisition to his mother. Since it was Saturday and the floors in the hall and the rooms had already been scrubbed for the Sunday, this prompted a quite understandable reaction from his mother. The black footprints on the white floor made her take a birch and beat the little culprit's legs. He was absolutely stunned by this attack because he did not understand what on earth he had done. He was shocked through and through and retreated crying into a corner.

Then his grandfather came to the rescue. Speaking mildly and with humour he fetched a bowl with water, soap and towel, and washed the little feet. Then he put them in socks and shoes and took his grandson for a walk to the next village. On the way he showed the child important features in the landscape, let him find answers to his own questions and so, with the help of the surroundings of nature and the kindness of his helping hand, he gently lifted the effects of the shock on his frightened soul. On the way back, however, in the dusk, his grandfather told the story of another boy who had been in a far worse situation because at the time of the great plague his parents and siblings had died and he was all alone in the big forest where the whole family had fled. After many weeks this little boy, after he had nursed a sick girl back to health, found his way back to his home village together with her and there became a respectable man.

All elements of curative-educational care for a child who is ill with fright or shock are joined here in the most beautiful way. There are no explanations necessary because if the basic tendency is understood, each event narrated in the story, each spoken word follows the course of healing.

In the evening, after the child had been put to bed, the day ended with his mother approaching him as he was almost asleep, and at this point the story reads:

> She made the sign of the cross on my forehead, mouth
> and breast. I knew that all was forgiven. Now blessed
> and relieved, I fell asleep ... When I was woken the sun
> shone through the window. It was a lovely Sunday,
> festive, after we said grace we had a breakfast feast.

Now everything that the day before had appeared as doom and gloom was solved and resolved. The misfortune of the cart grease had not been forgotten but transformed through the grandfather's kind wisdom.

The following story, 'Limestone,' which was printed for the first time in 1848 under the title 'The Poor Benefactor,' is about a different curative-educational problem. It is about a boy who grew up without a mother, together with his twin brother, guided by a kind yet very busy father. The brother is the 'other one' who overshadows the boy, because the 'other one' learns quickly and well and easily grows to assume the responsibilities of life. The boy himself, however, is not so bright, learns with difficulty and slowly and later, as an apprentice in his father's tannery, is always clumsy.

Soon the brother manages his father's company, but the boy, now a grown-up man, retreats into his room and starts all over again to work through the whole school material which he could not grasp when he was a child. With great effort he obtains a basic education and, to prove himself, even passes some examinations. He spends many years of his life doing this. In the meantime the father died, a romance was nipped in the bud, and finally the tannery managed by his brother runs into financial problems. It has to be sold, and the brother dies of shame at the loss. Now that he is free from the shadow of his brother the surviving one can thrive. He studies at a seminary and becomes a priest. In this capacity he goes to a very bleak and poor area and fulfils his duties there conscientiously and with dedication. He is aware of his limitations, his lack of intellect and weakness of mind. Yet, since he has found his place in life, he is in harmony with his environment and he retains the dignity of his human existence.

The way in which landscape and human destiny are joined together here, how an extraordinary being emerges from a previous situation, is told to perfection. What appears as a weakness of the hero's will-power and leads to inattentiveness, flights of fancy, clumsiness and indecision, is gradually overcome, and then a death facilitates a step which later affects the people of the whole parish — this course of events is in itself a fine picture of the effects of curative education. Through the example of his existence the priest, who is moderately disabled himself, becomes the curative educator of his community.

The following story, 'Tourmaline,' previously published in 1852 under the title 'The Gatekeeper of the Manor-House,' is about the break-up of a family which already from the start had been shaken in its foundations. First the father is described as an eccentric who, although still young, lives from his pension and hoards the most peculiar objects in his home. He has the typical traits of a kleptomaniac. It is not surprising that his wife starts an affair and turns to her husband's friend, a well-known actor. One day she disappears leaving her infant girl at her husband's house. He searches for the woman but cannot find even a trace of her, and so he takes the child and leaves the house where his life has gone to pieces.

Many years later these two have become strange characters. The father plays the flute in a number of taverns in Vienna; the girl has not attended school, speaks in incomprehensible words and sentences and spends her days in a small basement apartment in the house where her father is gatekeeper; the house itself is derelict. The rest of the story — the father dies in an accident, the girl by chance comes into the care of other people and regains parts of her humanity — needs to be read and studied in the original, because with great empathy Stifter describes the working of destiny, how it brings this strange pair to the narrating woman's attention and how again and again the narrator is taken by the hand and guided to the point where she eventually can become the carer and guardian of this girl.

The portrayal of the girl herself is full of understanding insight. The description of her speech impairment reveals an undeveloped sense of language, some kind of sensory aphasia which gradually recedes. The shyness of the child and her close attachment to a raven are traits of most distinct clarity, typical of a soul-life formed by neglect and incarceration. All this happened due to the father's strange disposition and the break-up of the family and only when the girl is included in family life can this be put right to some extent.

This masterpiece is followed by perhaps the best work of Stifter's art, 'The Rock Crystal.' It was published in 1846 under the title 'Christmas Eve' and found great admiration at the time. The plot is minimal. On Adam and Eve's Day, December 24, the two children of the shoemaker couple in the village go to the nearby market town to see their maternal grandparents, to bring presents and to take gifts with them. On the way back in the afternoon the boy, Konrad, and his little sister, Sanna, lose their way due to a sudden snowfall, and instead of going down into their home valley they walk up into the rocky glacier region of the mountains. Night falls and the two wandering children find a bare shelter in a cave. There the brother tries to keep his tired little sister awake because he knows that she might not survive the cold if she falls asleep.

Eventually the sun rises in the morning. 'A huge, gigantic blood-red disc rose from the snowy edges into the sky, and at that moment the snow round the children turned red as though strewn with millions of roses.' Christmas Day dawns, the day on which the children lost in the ice are rescued. The whole village had already started out at night to search for the children. Eventually Philipp, the shepherd, and a few others find the two children who do not quite understand what all the excitement is about and why the father is even lost for words when he takes them in his arms.

The immediate joy, the happiness of recovery and returning home is told in a way that echoes in a different form the story of the lost son. What is so moving, touching to the heart, without the need to articulate it, is the simple description of the two children who, in innocence, become Adam and Eve, lose the way to their parents' home and on Christmas Day are led home by the strength of a community of people who joined together 'at the right hour' coming to the rescue.

This is the archetype of all curative education: That the lost spirit-soul, which has taken the wrong way in glacial depths of the mind or the rocky faces of the body, is shown the way back to earth and guided by the strength of a community of people dedicated to this soul. This Christmas story highlights this course of action, and can again and again fill the heart with fresh courage and hope.

The last story, 'Katzensilber' or 'Fool's Gold' was at first titled 'The Brown Girl' after the main character of this strange story. It is not really about this girl but about a family in which three children, two girls and a little boy, grow up surrounded by their parents and paternal grandmother in a secure and quiet life. Into this storms, with cautious boisterousness, this brown child, half creature of nature, half human being; she is timid and wild, demanding and giving, open and reserved at the same time. At first she appears mute and uses gestures to communicate, and only gradually does she begin to trust and to speak. In a sudden hailstorm she saves the lives of the three children due to her foresight and alertness in assessing the situation. This experience brings her closer to the family, and she spends a few days in the house together with the children, but she always escapes into the forest again where she vanishes and cannot be found. No-one near or far knows her or where she lives. After a few years, when the family's house is on fire, she suddenly comes running from the forest and saves the life of the youngest son. From that time on she joins the life in the house, begins to learn together with the other girls, begins to open up and communicate and grows up together with the other children.

But then one day she is so overwhelmed by the distress caused by her loneliness and sense of strangeness that, despite all the affection and love she has received, she goes back to where she came from never to return. It remains unknown where she came from, there are only two hints that she is a creature of the magic world of the elements.

This human being has a lot in common with those children we describe as pre-psychotic today. Her foreignness to the world of people, the aloofness of her existence and her strange behaviour are portrayed in a masterly way. Especially her ambivalence, this desire for human company and warmth and the immediate retreat as soon as these qualities seem to have been secured, the intense approach combined with her coldness and insensitivity are a psychological masterpiece.

The tragic end of the story, the void and the sorrow she leaves behind, are similar to the feelings and emotions which we so often experience when living with these kinds of children.

Bunte Steine represents a kind of introductory course for curative education which can prepare the soul and the heart for this work and which will continue to be a source of advice and comfort. Adalbert Stifter's work, created on the strength of his humanitarianism, his sense of mercy and in anticipation of a new image of the human being, will still provide a companion for curative-educational work in years to come.

4

These five stories are a treasure trove of almost forgotten curative-educational knowledge and advice. They retain the last gleam of an insight into the nature of the human soul which seemed to be lost just a few years later. Alongside *Bunte Steine* are two other publications of the same period.

In 1845 *The Principles of Medical Psychology* by Ernst von Feuchtersleben appeared, and in the following year *Psyche* by Carl Gustav Carus was published. These two books are of a similar nature; they represent some of the last examples of a concept of the world and the human being which hardly stood a chance to develop to full existence. Because the upcoming agnostic natural science nipped in the bud what had strived to exist as Goetheanism at the start of the nineteenth century. In those days a new understanding of the human soul and the human mind was sought and a last, glowing reflection of this can still be found in these two books.

A similar reflection characterizes the *Bunte Steine*. For a long while these stories were the last artistic expression of the aspiration, to which Pestalozzi and Guggenbühl, Itard and Séguin and many others felt committed.

The aberrations in the soul-life of children are not described as incurable genetic properties of the central nervous system but as conditions which need care, guidance and inner schooling. If this is done the 'coloured gemstone' of the soul-spirit, which lies and has its effects in every human being, can be made to shine again. For Stifter this was a requirement for restoring the dignity of the human being.

Bunte Steine was followed by a dark period in the under-standing of the child's soul. Only at the start of the twentieth century were there glimmers of light. Then, when Rudolf Steiner held the twelve lectures of the Curative Education Course in 1924, it was as if windows had been opened wide to let the light of understanding for the abnormal soul-life flow into the sphere of the earth. Then the essential spiritual qualities of a curative educator were also described and much of what Stifter had anticipated presented itself with great clarity.

Rudolf Steiner seriously appealed for people to observe the 'gentle law' and urged curative educators to develop 'reverence for the small.' The respect for the human being, which Stifter knew to awaken through his narration, was now deepened and underpinned by the numerous insights conveyed by Rudolf Steiner. And the passage in the second lecture, 'Without allowing ourselves this religious feeling towards the cosmos, we cannot possibly develop a right attitude towards the child'[1] appealed to the qualities of the curative educator which Stifter implied in some of his characters.

There are many passages in these lectures where Rudolf Steiner gave instructions which are of utmost importance for the education of the educator himself. Thus he took up again what was striving to come into existence as true curative education at the beginning of the nineteenth century and what had been magically transformed in Stifter's book as a last revelation. This true curative education was awakened again by these twelve lectures in June and July 1924.

For this reason Rudolf Steiner was also able to say in this course:

> But the fact is, anyone who sets out to educate abnormal children will never have finished learning. Each single child will be for him a new problem, a new riddle. And the only way he can succeed in finding what he must do in the individual case is to let himself be guided by the being in the child. It is not easy, but it is the only real way to work. And this is the reason why it is of such paramount importance that, as teachers, we should take in hand our own self-education.
>
> The best kind of self-education will be found to consist in *following the symptoms of illness with interest,* so that we have the feeling: there is something quite wonderful about that symptom! ... We should ... be fully awake to the fact that when an abnormal symptom makes its appearance something is there which, seen spiritually, is nearer to the spiritual than the things that are done by man in his healthy organism ... If we have once grasped this, then many intimate truths will reveal themselves to us.[2]

Stifter anticipated this. The 'brown girl' in 'Fool's Gold' is much closer to spirituality than the three well-protected children who grow up rather placidly with no real contact to spirituality. And the disabled priest in 'Limestone' is of much greater devotion and piety than his gifted and intelligent brother. Thus each story conveys the appeal to see aberration as something that is closer to spirituality.

It was a deep love for the human being that led Adalbert Stifter to this first path of curative education. A few years after *Bunte Steine* was published Darwin's book, *The Origin of Species,* conquered the world. Its alternative title was *The Preservation of*

Favoured Races in the Struggle for Life. Here the opponent of all mercy and curative education raised his voice. At first he was stronger than 'the gentle law' and the 'reverence for the small.' But gradually the good is taking its course, and people see that not the struggle for life but the support for everything that is in need of soul care is striving to become the law of life.

Euthanasia

Two Lectures

Das Problem der

Euthanasie

1. Vortrag
am
1. November 1965
in
Föhrenbühl

Cover of Karl König's lecture manuscript
Föhrenbühl, November 1, 1965

11

The Problem of Euthanasia

Ladies and Gentlemen, dear Friends,

It is not unreasonable that on a day like today, when a large number of people commemorate those who have passed through the gateway of death, that on a day like this we want to make a genuine effort to reflect on such a significant historic issue like the problem of euthanasia. Because we all know, the younger ones perhaps not as well as us older ones, that in Central Europe millions of people have fallen victim to a misconceived euthanasia, that is, have been sent through the gateway of death by certain powers. So this problem of euthanasia belongs to those events which in this country are frequently described, to use a valid catchphrase, as the 'unresolved past.' And yet it will be necessary that this part of an unresolved past is gradually resolved. This cannot be done by holding trials and prosecuting although I do know that this is necessary. Also, there is absolutely no way — none at all — of doing it by starting an intellectual debate on what is right and what is wrong.

These events of an unresolved past have clearly and definitely shown that human existence, between the boundaries of birth and death, has no capacity of coping with this problem, or even getting closer to a solution, because the questions being asked address this problem in a completely inadequate way. And if the present generation does not understand that neither a dogmatic Christianity nor an intellectualized science is able to solve such a problem, if they are not prepared to understand in their hearts that through these approaches they not only cannot resolve this issue but that they are not even asking the right questions. With such approaches we will inevitably move towards a similar disaster as it has befallen humankind twenty-five years ago. I use such earnest words because things are much more serious than can actually be described or expressed. So much for an introduction.

And now to the issue of euthanasia. All of you surely know what the word euthanasia means although it is extremely difficult to describe or define what euthanasia is. Some may think of this, others may think of that. Some think of the legal trials they have read about, others think of the terrible things which have happened, a third group may think of euthanasia of severely ill people, and yet others may think of the annihilation of so-called life unworthy of living, of cripples, deformed or retarded people. All lies within the scope of the word euthanasia. It is a catch-all name and this is associated with the fact that year after year the problems of euthanasia are put in front of the people in various ways and forms. They swallow this, just as they swallow all problems these days — without digesting, and then forgetting them. Then they start to rumble about in the soul, come back to the surface and are suppressed again because it is actually so difficult to find a solution.

But, dear friends, first of all we should take a look at a historic aspect which, although it is often forgotten about, is intimately connected with the problem of euthanasia and this is the following. At the turn of the fifth to the fourth pre-Christian century, when Hippocrates stepped out of the mystery schools in Kos and became the founder of European medicine, something came about that is valid to this day, namely the Hippocratic oath. It is still valid for the simple reason that nothing better and more appropriate has been found. What is actually the subject of the Hippocratic oath? It is priestly medicine, something that had been appropriate earlier. With the Hippocratic oath the priest's power over the life and death of those who had entrusted themselves to him was broken. And if I read some of it you will see what I mean.

> 3. I will apply dietetic measures for the benefit of the sick according to my ability and judgment; I will keep them from harm and injustice.
>
> 4. I will neither give a deadly drug to anybody who asked for it, nor will I make a suggestion to this effect. Similarly I will not give to a woman an abortive remedy. In purity and holiness I will guard my life and my art.
>
> 7. What I may see or hear in the course of the treatment or even outside of the treatment in regard to the life of people, which on no account one must spread abroad, I will keep to myself, holding such things shameful to be spoken about.

These are some, today still valid, passages of the Hippocratic oath which we, those of us who are doctors, have vowed to keep.

But the times of Hippocratic medicine are over. This time of Hippocratic medicine came to an end at the historic moment when, for example, a man like Samuel Hahnemann made a completely new approach to medical thinking and medical practice. This approach, which came about exactly 2 100 years after Hippocrates, was not accepted. As a result the Hippocratic thinking (namely the thinking of elements — air, water, earth, fire — and their effects on the world and on the human being which form the foundation of Hippocrates' pathology) was gradually lost. Something completely new, a necessarily materialistic medicine, filled the void that was left. And this medicine, which is based on science and is no longer entitled to call itself the art of healing, has assumed this oath.

But this oath is not valid any more. The oath is no longer valid because the time of this holy oath belongs to the past. Something completely different has happened. Something of which you can say that, as in the fifth and fourth centuries BC, when in Kos Hippocrates opened up the medical mysteries, so now the time has come that new medical mysteries open up, not in the twilight of the temple but in the awakening spiritual light of those human souls who are ready for it. I would like to repeat that with the appearance of Hahnemann the medical era of Hippocrates came to an end. Hahnemann was not accepted and as a result something else emerged to replace what Hahnemann was to have achieved.

The emergence of materialistic medicine was inevitable, but then another step was taken in order to pursue further what had been started by Hahnemann, and this was done by none other than Rudolf Steiner. Through him the medical mysteries opened up again, medical mysteries which give an insight into the true image of the human being which today should again guide therapy and healing based on many of Hahnemann's teachings. And historically it is extraordinarily interesting that at the same moment, that is in 1920 when Rudolf Steiner held his first course for a group of about thirty-five doctors, the Medusa's head of euthanasia rose again and made its presence known. It is very interesting what the American writer Pearl S. Buck — who has a retarded child herself and wrote a small, very moving book about this — said about the word euthanasia, that it was nice and gentle sounding, but concealed its threat as all gentle sounding words do. And what was the situation in 1920 when the Medusa's head of euthanasia appeared before humanity?

In that year two little books were published. One of them was written by a man called Gerhard Hoffmann under the pseudonym of Ernst Mann, and was entitled *Die Moral der Kraft* (the morality of might), and the second, by Karl Binding, an important, great lawyer, was entitled *Die Freigabe der Vernichtung lebensunwerten Lebens* (allowing the destruction of unworthy life). The first one was a book written by a young man and based on a concept that was quite racial. The other one was the result of an entire life, because Binding died in the same year in which this text was published. It needs to be added that Binding was an extraordinary and respectable person. In law he represented

morality and in some way it is quite upsetting to read in this con-
cluding booklet written at the end of his life, how he struggled
with this problem. He could not understand, guided by his
moral beliefs, why it was possible that such people who were
unable to take responsibility for themselves, who may not even
have had awareness, who spoke in a confused manner and dis-
played antisocial behaviour, why it should not be possible to end
the life of those people. He even says at the end of his booklet
that 'the good and sensible need to happen despite all risks of
mistakes.' This means therefore that even if we are at times mistaken and kill someone for no reason the good and sensible still
needs to be done for people and for humankind. This book was
reprinted in 1922, this time with an epilogue by Hoche, a psychiatrist and at least as well-known and famous as the author.

And in the same year, in 1922, another book by Gerhard
Hoffmann was published called *Die Erlösung der Menschheit vom
Elend* (the redemption of humankind from misery). In this
book, similar to Hoche's and Binding's writing, there is the following, which I will quote as the problem really needs to be
described in detail. The following demands are made:

> 1. Painless destruction of all mentally ill people, also
> of those who have lost their self-determination, are
> subjected to an incurable lingering illness and whose life
> is a burden for themselves and for others.
> 2. Euthanasia for all those dying people who are in
> agony and cannot be saved from death.
> 3. Euthanasia for all who are suicidal and who, in
> order to escape unbearable emotional and physical
> suffering, want to end their life voluntarily.
> 4. Painless killing of young children soon after birth if
> they are born crippled or with incurable diseases.[1]

If you read things like this and consider them on the basis of
present-day thinking and perception you might as well say, is
this not a valid point? And you may well follow Binding's

conclusion when he describes the 'incurable idiots' (words like
this were used in those days):

> They have neither the will to live nor to die and as a
> result, as far as they are concerned, there is no notable
> consent to their death, on the other hand this killing
> does not come up against a will to live which needs to be
> broken. Their life is absolutely meaningless yet they do
> not feel that it is unbearable. For their families as well as
> for society they are a terrible burden. Their death does
> not leave the smallest gap [note this argumentation!]
> except perhaps in the feelings of the mother or devoted
> carer. [And now the lawyer speaks] Again I can find
> from a legal or social, from a moral or religious
> standpoint, virtually no reason for not allowing the
> destruction of these people who present the appalling
> counter-image of real people and who horrify almost
> everyone who encounters them — of course not by
> anyone. In times of higher morality — nowadays all
> heroism has been lost — the authorities would allow the
> freeing of these poor people from themselves.[2]

Contemplating something like that you begin to understand
the attitude which evolves from it. This is not at all an unusual
moral attitude. This man is right! He is right according to the
ideas of the nineteenth century which then pervaded human
existence. He cannot look at something abnormal, misshapen
and deformed; it needs to be pushed away. From the same conduct, yet from different layers of the soul, appears, for example,
what in someone like Hoffmann is motivated by nationalism
and racism: a humanity that is beautiful, noble, wonderful, athletic, straightforward, blond and blue-eyed. With Hoche it is different again. In the same year, in 1922, when he republished
Binding's writing, he spoke at the psychiatrists' congress in the
south of Baden, saying:

Never is the spiritual world present as a whole; it always and everywhere is only present as the intellectual property of an individual. It always develops afresh in the brain and then disappears again. The existence of a real spiritual world is one of the great illusions which are so abundant in our life.[3]

This is Hoche. If you believe this, if you believe that the existence of a real spiritual world 'is one of the great illusions which are so abundant in our life,' so that actually nothing exists beyond the thinking which is trapped between birth and death, then how could you possibly oppose this issue of euthanasia? Is it not an *eu-thanatos,* a glorified death, if I administer an injection to someone in agony so that he dies and is free of pain, if I help a lunatic or a criminal pass through the gateway of death so that the people around him are protected? If I just provide a so-called painless death for deformed children who are only going to be a burden to their parents, siblings and relatives?

Do you see how the era of Hippocrates has come to an end? A man of the eighteenth, seventeenth, or fifteenth century would never have dared to think such thoughts because the church still had some moral power, because the family was still a factor in everyday life. Since the end of the First World War this has changed. Whoever does not begin to see this, is turning a blind eye to the enormous threats to which humanity is exposed today because there is a vacuum and anything can flood and flow into this vacuum if it is not filled with new insights. What Hoffmann, Hoche and Binding expressed as ideas in 1920 and 1922 turned into action twenty years later. Action which is in fact beyond comprehension. After the invasion of Poland in October 1940 Adolf Hitler wrote a letter which was later backdated to September 1, 1939:

Reichsleiter Bouhler and Dr Brandt, are charged with the responsibility of extending the authority of certain to be named physicians in such a manner that persons who, according to human judgment, are incurable can, upon a most careful diagnosis of their condition of sickness, be accorded a mercy death.

(signed) A. Hitler[4]

This letter unleashed the devil. Not only doctors and psychiatrists but also judges and prosecutors made themselves available, and with this letter Operation Gnadentod (mercy killing) commenced and spread over Germany for approximately one and a half years. As early as autumn 1939 all curative and care institutes received the following questionnaires:

Regarding the requirement of compiling a record of curative and care institutes for economic planning purposes, you are requested by return to complete and send back the attached questionnaire with reference to the enclosed notes.

Report all patients who:

1. suffer from the following illnesses and cannot be occupied in the institute workplaces or can only be given repetitive tasks (plucking and similar):

schizophrenia,

epilepsy (state cause if exogenic, war wound or other),

senile illnesses,

therapy-refractory paralysis and other syphilitic diseases,

disability of all kinds,

encephalitis,

Huntington disease;

or 2. who have been in institutes for at least five years;

or 3. are retained as criminally insane;

or 4. are not of German nationality or not of German or related blood, stating their race and nationality.[5]

This, too, I need to read sentence by sentence and word by word because it is essential that we know such things if we want to consider them. You see, in Germany in those days there was a large group of doctors and carers who protested, refusing to answer this questionnaire. Yet there was another group who through weakness, apathy or conviction completed this questionnaire. According to present estimates (I cannot verify this) approximately 70 000 to 80 000 people were victims of this questionnaire in 1940 and 1941. We should remember these people because they went through extraordinary suffering. For many of them it was not *eu-thanasia* at all, because the government department, Reichsstelle T4, instructed the annihilation centres to do it as cheaply as possible, by for example, reducing spending on food to twenty or twenty-five pfennig per day so that these people gradually died of starvation. In time furnaces had to be built behind these institutes because of the great number of victims. The same department wrote letters to the parents and families that their child, husband or wife, their sister, brother, mother, father or son had suddenly contracted pneumonia, and despite the best medical help available it had unfortunately been impossible to save them; because of the danger of an epidemic it would not be possible to come for the body; could they advise where to send the ashes. These letters were so odious and the still reasonable people of that time were so incensed that Operation Gnadentod had to be called off in 1942. But those who had proved their proficiency at these annihilation centres were transferred to Auschwitz and other death camps to put into practice on a much larger scale what they had learned.

Compared to this the trials being held today are completely irrelevant. For something like this there is only one way of dealing with it: to ask how it is possible that in the middle of Germany, in the middle of Central Europe, in Austria, in Bohemia, in Poland, in Holland such things could happen. And this is the point we need to reflect, namely that where the foundations of faith have become irrelevant, where the foundations of Christianity no longer exist, where human life is seen only between birth and death and everything else is dismissed with a cynical smile, that from there it is only one step away from unleashing the underworld. That those people in whom something had been unleashed are now condemned in court, is because the Bindings and the Hoches had preached this intellectualism and were respectable men who had state funerals. That is what gradually needs to be understood in order to resolve the past. It is not the henchmen — they are to be pitied because they have to live with the destiny of those who were killed — but those who have made them henchmen, who at the same time crucified what had been left of Christianity, they are important. And the question is: What can we do?

Dear friends, there is only one thing we can do. And that is to remember every day and every hour to overcome what Luther had called *massa carnis,* a heap of flesh, at the sight of a retarded child, to overcome every day and every hour the mistaken idea that aberration, deformity, pain, misery, suffering are needless. Because only if we constantly try to transform this in our soul, if we start an inner process — not in others but in each and every one of us for ourselves — something will be brought about. We shall gradually see birth and death not as two events which happen only once at the start and the end of our life, but that birth and death are continuous events within us. That in fact the birth of a human being is not over with the child being delivered into the earthly world from the waters of the mother, and that life is not over when the heart suddenly stops and breathing ceases. But that there is a process, a constant process of birth continuing from the beginning to the end of life, and a continuous process of death which has its effects from the end of life back to its beginnings. If we really begin to be serious about a word like incarnation and excarnation, that actually a gradual incarnation into the body is taking place and that at the same time excarnation is a gradual death.

There is a reason why Rudolf Steiner spoke of a threefold birth. The birth of the physical body at the moment when the child is released from the mother's body into the world; this is the very first birth. Then incarnation continues until the age when the first change of form takes place and the second teeth break through, when the child reaches school age. Then this second birth happens and the etheric body, the body of formative forces is born. This body of formative forces now begins to activate, harmonize and individualize what was there as the physical disposition of walking, speaking and thinking, and this continues through school age, develops further, grows, changes, metamorphoses until adolescence. Then a third birth takes place and that is the one when the astral body frees itself from the mother's fold, when a kind of internalization takes place in the young person, when they begin to live with their own and not someone else's feelings, when they begin to speak their own language, when they gradually begin to meet their own destiny, and become their own human being. Until in their twenty-first year, mature, they begin to stand in the world on their own. But then the process of birth continues internally, the various soul members transform, become sentient soul, later mind soul, become consciousness soul, a constant process of being born sets in.

This is a continual process through the whole of human life, and in the same way the process of death reaches from the end of our existence to its beginning. We could not live without beginning to die right from the start. Even the first signs of consciousness in a baby, the first blink of an eye, the first being aware of the world, taking in, perceiving the environment, all this is only possible because processes of death, processes of dying take place in the human organism. Because bones harden, because urine is produced, because faeces is excreted, because bile is produced, everything which is a process of reduction and excretion is a process of death. And on the other side there is the beginning of enlightenment, consciousness develops, pain is experienced, needs make themselves known, forces need to be overcome. Do you realize what this is about?

To empower a person to suffer his destiny, to stand by a person yet at the same time knowing, this is his destiny. This means to enable a person to die already during his life, because he can only become a human being, not to mention taking control of himself, if he begins to strive towards further inner development. If he does not solely choose to meet people because of sympathy or antipathy, if he does not go to sleep and wakes up again on his whim but that he gradually takes control of his own processes of death. That he learns to think what he himself wants to think, that he transforms his feelings in order to encounter people objectively, that he outgrows himself within the death process of his existence. 'He who does not die before dying will perish when he dies,' Angelus Silesius said. And there are Goethe's wonderful words: 'As long as you have not grasped this: "Die, and be transformed!" you will be nothing but a sombre guest on the dark earth.' Dying needs to be learned so that we, when the time comes, can do it. Being born, that is given to us.

And what is euthanasia actually doing? It is indeed terrible quackery, that is, it is a delusion. Euthanasia aims to extinguish the light of human existence and the lights of lives instead of kindling the lights of the spirit. We can envision this in a kind of picture, this path of incarnation from birth to death, this path of excarnation from death having its effect on birth. From Rudolf Steiner we hear that there is the gate of the moon, and in the same way that the moon shines down on us it symbolizes the gateway of birth through which we step into life; and as the sun shines in the sky it symbolizes for us the gateway of death through which we pass. The gate of the moon and of birth determines our course according to the laws of necessity. Through the gate of the sun, however, a ray of freedom shines onto us which — if only we learn the right way to die in every moment — we will be able to awaken. If one begins to live with views like this then something like these phantoms of euthanasia will be utterly defeated by words like those of Rudolf Steiner:

> We must acquire a definite, concrete view of the divine.
> And this we do when we recognize, for example, the
> deep connection of the moon with our own past, indeed
> with the past of the whole earth. Then, when we look at
> the moon in the heavens, we can say, 'You cosmic being
> of necessity, when I contemplate that within me over
> which my will has no sway, I feel inwardly united with
> you.' ...
>
> If in the same way we contemplate the inmost nature
> of the sun, our whole humanity within cosmic existence
> is connected to the existence of the sun, and we can feel
> in saying to the sun, 'You cosmic being of freedom, I feel
> inwardly united with you when I contemplate everything
> in me that gives freedom and the ability to make
> decisions for the future.'[6]

Then we can learn to see ourselves as standing between necessity and freedom, not into necessity alone but between this gate of the moon and this gate of the sun which enlightens the whole of our life. And at the gate of necessity, for example, those incarnation problems occur which we see in children in need of soul care, in insane people, in all those souls who cannot find their way in this life, and we see in old, frail, poor souls who are unable to die that they cannot reach this freedom of the sun gate.

If we can see all this, then we begin to understand that we need to aquire quite different ideas to meet the future image of the human being, and to meet the mystery medicine on whose basis a new Hippocratic oath is not sworn but can come to life in the heart of everyone, not just in the heart of the doctor. Then, perhaps we will be able to see even the most crippled, deformed, or the most maltreated body as a countenance formed by necessity, with all its wrinkles and lines, its scars and deformities, into which the necessities of destiny are inscribed. But in such a countenance there may be a glance, the glimmer of freedom, however small it might be, that begins to shine and then a growing understanding is kindled in the human heart: I must not kill. Because although I have been given the power to do this, I have been imbued from the sun with the power of the freedom of dying. This power prevents me from using what I have been given as a human being, as a kin of Cain. I must surrender this power which was given to me. And at the moment that this happens today in individual people something else immediately comes to mind. People begin to experience that today the whole of humankind has to go through the same temptation as Jesus Christ did during the forty days in the wilderness after the baptism in the Jordan. There Lucifer approached him and showed him all the kingdoms of the world, saying, 'Take them, they are yours.' Rudolf Steiner describes this in the *Fifth Gospel:*

> First, the Christ being within the body of Jesus encountered Lucifer in the loneliness — Lucifer with all his power and influence, who draws near to men when they prize the self too highly and are lacking humility and self-knowledge. To play upon the false pride, the tendency to self-aggrandisement in man — that is Lucifer's aim. Now he confronted Christ Jesus and spoke roughly as recorded in the other Gospels: Behold me! The other kingdoms into which man's life has been set, the foundations of which were laid by the primeval gods and spirits — these kingdoms have grown old. I will establish a new kingdom. If you will enter my realms, I will give you all the beauty and the glory which belong to these old kingdoms. But you must sever yourself from the other gods and acknowledge me!
>
> And Lucifer described all the glories of his world, everything that speaks to the human soul if it has only a little price. But the Christ being came from the spiritual worlds and knew who Lucifer is, knew how souls must

resist if they are not to be led astray by Lucifer on earth. Untouched as he was by this temptation, the Christ being knew how the gods are truly served, and he had the power to repel the onslaught of Lucifer.[7]

Humankind should become strong enough to reject Lucifer, to reject him in the way that Jesus Christ once did in the desert. This face of Lucifer, this is the face of euthanasia which comes up to us and confronts us today.

Dear friends, this is what I wanted to say tonight. There may be another evening in November when we can talk about the problem of euthanasia from a different perspective, the perspective of the social community.

12

Euthanasia as a Challenge
to Society Today

Dear Friends,

It is good and also necessary that today we address again this whole problem which is so vaguely described as the problem of euthanasia. Last time I mentioned that when you use this word, people have many different ideas about it. On November 1, we tried to take a first look at the whole problem from the perspective of the individual. We considered, for example, the Hippocratic oath because for the last 2500 years the physician's task in society was first and foremost to heal the individual person. This will have to change in the centuries to come but this was the situation until now. And with this consideration of euthanasia and the individual human being, we approached the basic problem which we described in this way — I am briefly recapitulating — that we referred to the gate of the moon, the gateway of birth, and to the gate of the sun, the gateway of death.

We simply concluded that a solution cannot be found as long as humankind is not prepared to pass through these gates consciously, that is, not to see human life as just taking place between birth and death. Instead humankind must learn to see individual human existence as reaching beyond birth and death, and that each of us comes from a spiritual existence, passes through life, and enters the spiritual world again through death.

As long as this is not taken into account, as long as this is not open for consideration, a real solution of the problem of euthanasia is basically impossible.

We concluded by connecting this with the eternal problem of all human existence which can be described with the words 'necessity and freedom.' We are born out of the necessity of our previous existence, our destiny. This necessity which outlines our earthly existence continuously kindles an element of freedom in us, the freedom to make decisions, the freedom to come to a resolve. With what we have gained as freedom stimulated by necessity we pass through the gate of the sun, the gate of brightness, the gate of light, to what awaits us as life after death. This is an image, dear friends, which immediately makes clear that one can no longer speak of a mercy death provided to one or the other person, because within the limitations of our human consciousness, within the necessary limitations of our existence we simply do not have the capacity to decide who should live and who should not. This is not for us to decide. And only if we clearly understand that the gate of birth and the gate of death are passages, only then will we be able to abandon dogmatic ideas and, as human beings on the strength of our clear and free resolve, we will have to categorically say 'No' to any such suggestions. That is the one side.

But there is also another side to the whole problem, that is not just the side of the individual, but also that side which is constantly being put forward: the human being within the community of people, the human being within his race, his people, his nation, his family. We want to try to approach the question from this side today. From this side the points frequently brought up, that people think that the ill, weak and disabled outgrowths of a healthy social organism simply need to be eliminated. Then it is easy to talk about maintaining the purity of people and race. Today the word 'race' is avoided but the word 'people' or 'nation' is emphasized, in the belief that this refers to something which is still real. And if people want to appear particularly modern they do not even refrain from adding economic considerations to the whole issue, thinking, for example, of the millions each state has to pay for such individuals, elderly, ill, confused, lost, retarded and crippled people in order to nourish, care for, rehabilitate and look after them. People believe that the economic case needs to be made, that it may be better for so-called normal people (politely called the working population) to be freed from such burdens.

It is interesting to read in the fine little book by Ehrhardt, a psychiatrist in Marburg, which has recently been published, what he has to say about this issue which I have only outlined just now. He discusses Catel's book:

> The organized and stable democratic state [as Catel calls it] could provide sufficient protection against the misuse of such a law [annihilation of unworthy life] against the annihilation of racially, politically and economically 'unwanted' life. But even the most constitutional procedure could not resolve the deeply questionable 'selection,' the problem of judging about the unworthiness of life in an individual case. The old as well as the new supporters of 'limited euthanasia' *both make the crucial mistake of regarding the worthiness of life as a fact which can be empirically-scientifically defined.* Against this is the fact that the worthiness of someone's life can only partially be the subject of medical diagnosis and prognosis because to a great extend it is beyond all empirical-scientific understanding. For the doctor this means that, by giving an overall assessment of the worthiness of someone's life, he is constantly breaching the limitation of his professional competence which is imposed on him by his factual knowledge. He should recognize the problem of such breaches, should be wary of them and above all should not put himself forward to judge the situation.[1]

These are clear words although they are not really an answer. Because what is said here is solely based on the common moral understanding of an individual as long as it is intact. Not the young ones among you, but we older ones have experienced how easily millions of people can abandon such a moral understanding out of wrong idealism, through persuasion, for many reasons, and then it is no longer presumed to be true what Ehrhardt describes here clearly, objectively and accurately. For this reason it is vitally important that people acquire new principles which may prove to be more durable than the morality living until now in every decent human being.

We need to make clear to ourselves that nowadays there are different rules, different moral values than in the past. For example, for the Teutons and for the Greeks two to three thousand years ago, euthanasia was common practice. The children, if they were a little deformed, were simply abandoned in the mountains. This was considered as something normal. For the Jews, even for those who lived in the third and second pre-Christian centuries, it was normal that firstborns were abandoned at particular locations because it was thought to be a requirement for making the family bonds stronger. People thought that the number of children, for example, would increase by sacrificing the first child under certain conditions. And still today there are tribes in Japan where it is considered normal that the old people, those over sixty whose teeth are starting to become loose, have a ceremonial meal with their family on a particular day of the year and next morning the eldest son carries the old father or mother in a tub to the top of the highest peak and leaves them where they sit awaiting starvation and the death which the elements bring. This is normal as long as the people, the tribe is a unified organism, when all parts of this tribe or people are still of the same blood, when sons and daughters and grandchildren and grandfathers are still of the same flesh, where there are still shared memories, shared experiences, where individuality is in fact of only marginal significance, and the tribe as a whole is still embedded in the tribal spirituality of a higher existence. There an element can be cut off like a brittle finger, that is still normal.

But from the moment when the Eucharist was celebrated for the first time, when flesh and blood were no longer tied to the tribe but to the spirit, that is to say from the moment when Christian communities were formed transcending ties of flesh and blood, of tribe, but were committed to the Eucharist, from this moment on, principles of humanity come into existence which needed to be newly defined. From this moment on if you talk about purity of race and racial organism you need to be aware that you are falling back into an antiquated past and remain ignorant of what has really happened to humanity since Jesus Christ came into the world. From then onwards human individuality gradually evolved, merging from the context of family, people or even race. And everything which happens these days in such a disastrous way — think of South America, of Africa, of Asia, especially of those Asian tribes in the Malayan archipelago — all these are the desperate birth-pangs of an individual humanity wanting to find itself, which is still so deeply embedded in its own racial existence that a battle erupts between the racial, tribal roots and a superficial intellectual individuality. The outer battle, war, revolution, desperation or murder is just an expression of what is going on between individuality and racial ties in each one of these people.

But we are living at a different level of history and today even these points are no longer valid. Even the battle between brave churchmen — both Catholic and Protestant — and the antiquated barbarism prevalent in Germany in the 1940s, still continued at the level of Christianity versus nationalism or race. Today, as can be seen from Ehrhardt's explanations, this would no longer catch on. When I say this I mean that it is no longer in tune with our circumstances. And this is because over the last thirty or forty years we have developed into an essentially completely new and unknown society.

If people look back in a hundred or even two hundred years' time to the social changes in the twentieth century they will see that since the start of the century and then at a rapidly increasing pace, something completely new came about in society. Because today we are surrounded by what can be called an increasingly affluent mass society. A society of affluent masses which actually pervades all levels of existence and all forms of social existence. Boundaries of the family, of nationality, of the tribe are practically non-existent in modern society. What still remains as relics of a former age — aristocracy and the like — all this is actually gone because this affluence has found its way into all social classes. Servants and masters, that is bygone. And even if, for example, socialist politicians still believe that they represent the working classes then this is a delusion because today even the petit bourgeois does not really exist, instead there is a society of the masses which gradually, we could say, disappears in prosperity. That is one thing.

Secondly, together with this — and it is difficult to say whether the one depends on the other as both are closely interconnected — we see a global population explosion on a scale which is virtually beyond grasp. Each year millions upon millions of people are born, and despite all considerations this deluge of people increasingly floods the earth. It would be ridiculous to say this is good and equally ridiculous to say it is bad; one can only describe it. What has happened? The disintegration of all order, the disintegration of the family, of ethnicity, of nations, has led to the dams that previously regulated births, the descent of human beings to earth, and regulated death, these dams have broken. Now a deluge of people sweeps over mountains and valleys, everywhere over the earth. Nobody can deny that.

And a third element is closely related to this which is the industrial overproduction that is now a necessity beyond all reason. Billions upon billions of articles are produced, no matter what, regardless whether they are needed or not. The balance of supply and demand as an overall regulating principle of economics has broken down. Goods are produced, supplied and put on the market because ever more efficient machines produce more and more. Believe me, because so much is produced this production activity affects consumers. The global economy has come to a stage where it affects consumers in such a way as an alarming example in the last two weeks has shown. I think it was November 4 or 5, when there was thick fog in the Rhineland. Despite the fact that visibility was reduced to a few metres, drivers continued racing along the autobahn at a speed of 100 and 120 kilometres per hour. The police were completely powerless in the situation, and within a few hours forty people died and hundreds of people were injured on a short stretch of the road. When they were asked, 'Why did you drive so fast?' the only answer was, 'Because the driver in front of me and the one behind me drove as fast, and if I had slowed down somebody else would have overtaken me and I could not be left behind.'

This was the typically German argument: I could not be left behind. Do you see what this is? It is mass society controlled by the power of a machine and the complete inability, because the will has become so weak, to counter this.

A few days ago, through a large part of the north-eastern United States and eastern Canada, there was a power failure and all lights went out suddenly. For twelve hours in New York people were trapped in the subways, were stuck in elevators, there was mayhem, muggings and murder in pitch-dark streets. One really should consider this and not just quickly read over it without further thought, because these are signs for us so that we can think about what is needed today. Millions upon millions of people function because power stations are still working. If, however, suddenly this enormous amount of electric power which flows through these huge networks, if this enormous power suddenly begins to flicker, then life comes to a standstill. Then this is the end of all morality. Then it's all over.

This shows that we are moving away from former human

bonds of blood, nature and soil — and in no way should we return to these — and that we are moving towards being a mass society bound together by the power of electricity, magnetism and machines. If there are no forces to counterbalance this then humanity on earth is finished. In this saturated mass society, which has generated a sea of productivity, two basic tendencies are emerging. One tendency is towards centralization. And together with this, simultaneously there is the opposite tendency of specialization. In a way we are all in the process of subjecting ourselves to concentration, each of us specializing as much as possible. Out of this comes the drive which can be found all over the world, but is strongest in North America and Germany, the drive to centralization, one the worst ills you can imagine. Centralization in government means that Washington or Bonn take over everything, that everything is decided there, that from there the whole country is operated. Social centralization means that trade unions are formed which are among the worst businesses we have today. Did you know that in Britain, for example, the trade unions do not know what to do with all the accumulated capital which they have taken from the workers? And then centralization in economy is seen in these giant multinational enterprises such as Unilever, ICI, Mannesmann, Krupp and many others which basically replace the ruling dynasties. For this reason there are giant department stores, giant ministries, giant hospitals today. Everything is as big as possible, everything is as concentrated as possible, forming a huge entity, whether it is in academia, in the economy or in government no longer matters. Gigantic buildings are erected — this is what homes look like today, what hospitals look like, what ministries look like, what factories look like — you cannot tell the difference any more. This is the result of the huge centralization and concentration, and inside this, specialization needs to develop because no-one, not even a group of people, is really able to oversee the whole thing.

So the individual becomes part of a gigantic system, becomes ever more specialized, and is surrounded by other specialists, and these are the two things which matter. To use an analogy you could say, in there everything is broken down, becomes specialized, becomes smaller and smaller. What I have illustrated here for you is basically the head. You see, Rudolf Steiner once pointed out that the head organization represents in us the powers of synthesis and that the lower organization represents the powers of analysis. In the head there is a massive organ, the brain whose function is synthesis, co-operation. In our body there is a diverse variety of organs, glands, etc. If we look at our arms, hands, fingers, feet, toes, this is all about differentiation, specialization. Now you see, in our economy of today the head, the giant corporation, has become more and more powerful, so big in fact that its limbs as specialist organs, which specialize more and more, have been shrivelled. If you know about Rudolf Steiner's views of medicine you will immediately recognize that this is a tumour growth. You could also say that it is nothing but the growth of an overly powerful social homonculus who is standing his ground everywhere today.

All this is the premise — and I am only now arriving at this topic — for what we now have to say about euthanasia. Because it seems to me that this sick social organism, this terminally ill social organism, this dying social organism is a massive cancerous tumour that is disintegrating. Like every sick organism it needs to be regulated. Whenever we are ill our body regulates itself by developing counterbalances. For example, a temperature is a counterbalance. Sweating, having diarrhea, are all counterbalances for something which is ill. And similar counterbalances need to develop in the ill social organism. Two counterbalances have emerged and developed especially in the last thirty or forty years while this cancerous tumour has become ever bigger and powerful, while our affluent society has become ever stronger, and the population explosion and industrial production have increased. Now two counterbalances have appeared.

One counterbalance is represented by the old people, the overly old people, those who cannot die because they are somehow kept alive. If you look at the statistics of this increase of the proportion of old people to others, then if this continues, you can see the extraordinary scenario that in all civilized countries people over sixty will soon form a third of the population. That is one thing.

The other counterbalance that has developed is what we are dealing with now, with the children, young people and adults who cannot be integrated into our society and economy of today. As a result of this, two completely new fields of science have developed over the last fifteen years: gerontology — the medical field concerned with understanding old and ageing people, pathologically, psychologically, in every way — and the completely new developing science of child psychiatry. This needs to be considered, and not simply accepted as given. It is not simply given, but is an expression of the two counterbalances which want to have an effects.

The counterbalance of children and adults in need of soul care is looming like a huge, ever growing crowd over the gate of the moon and birth. Because these are all human souls who can only find their way into life with great difficulty, who seek the path of incarnation but who cannot yet join today's life and today's existence because of disorders of the body and the soul. And at the other side, at the gate of death there looms this huge crowd of old and overly old people, and this is an issue of excarnation. They are those who stand waiting, knocking at the gate of death but who cannot find the way in. This is what calls upon those who think of everything in terms of economics, race, genetics. This is the call at the gate of birth and at the gate of death. But if the thinking merely happens as it is does today, half consciously, half unconsciously, then it will simply lead to unplanned absurdity. Then the fever would be treated instead of the illness, the inflammation instead of the cause, in the simplistic belief that this is healing.

Many phenomena of the carnival of life seen today are the struggle and efforts to cope with this all-pervading craze of centralization which has retracted the limbs and the rhythmic system, breathing and heartbeat. Just look at these hysterical young people in their tens of thousands shaking, kicking, and screaming to welcome the Beatles or other pop stars. What do they really want? They are trying to kick their limbs out of this giant head, but are not really successful. Or if you look on the road and see how the drivers inevitably retract into the head of their car and then let this head move and drive, then you will be able to see the same picture everywhere. But then there are the counterbalances — the old people, the retarded, the manic, psychotic and disabled ones. Our task is not to approach these people with negative euthanasia, but to learn that there is something completely different.

There is something which I would venture to call *positive euthanasia*. This is something which is beginning to awaken in young people today. In America the Peace Corps working for developing countries is positive euthanasia. Curative education as a support in life is positive euthanasia. Building old peoples' homes, as misguided as it may be, is an attempt of positive euthanasia. It is an attempt of taking community-forming seeds from these counterbalances and putting them into the cancer-inflicted organism of our society. This is what it is about.

Euthanasia must not be allowed to be a mercy killing. That is quackery, human, religious, social, downright quackery. Instead we need to set a positive euthanasia of new communities against this. It is as if the royal wedding is not attended by those who were invited, and instead everyone from the streets is invited to attend. For at present the main issue is to build these communities, even if they are small, and to build them where at the gate of death and at the gate of birth the counterbalances are in waiting. In 1921, forty-five years ago, Rudolf Steiner said the following to young people:

In the future it will be said that all the tasks of the
individual will become tasks of the community, and that
tasks of the community must become one's own. Only
this will work, but you cannot organize that; it must be
associated.

These are strange words, dear friends, because today we are in
a situation where every task of the individual is the task of the
community, and that is how he wants it to be; but we are not yet
in a situation where each individual makes the tasks of the community his own.

In the old people, in the ill, the psychotic, the frail, the disabled ones there is one thing we can experience, and that is the
nature of the human being. We need to learn to look at it in wonder. It needs to kindle compassion in us, and wonder and compassion need to create the conscience that will lead us to the
formation of a new community, and that means to serve the
growing Christ impulse. And positive euthanasia is a healing
impulse, and this healing impulse is a profound impulse which
cannot be represented by an individual doctor but only by a
community of healers who want to represent it.

And this healing impulse bears Paracelsus' words which say
about this will to heal:

> In the heart he grows
> Out of God he comes
> He is of natural light
> The highest of all healing substance
> Is love.

This, essentially, is positive euthanasia.

Notes

Preface

1 Strohschein, 'Die Entstehung der anthroposophischen Heilpädagogik,' pp. 216ff.
2 Arnim, 'Was bedeutet Seelenpflege?' pp. 27ff.
3 Müller-Wiedemann, *Karl König,* p. 181.
4 Heidenreich, 'Dr Karl König,' *Christian Community Journal,* 1966, p. 129.
5 See p. 54.
6 Asperger, *Heilpädagogik.*
7 König, 'Wahre und falsche Wege in der Heilpädagogik.'
8 Steiner, *Geschichtliche Symptomatologie.*
9 König, 'Das Problem der Euthanasie,' p. 3.
10 See Petersen & Zankel, 'Werner Catel – ein Protagonist der NS-Kindereuthanasie und seine Nachkriegskarriere.' *Medizinhistorisches Journal. Medicine and the Life Sciences in History,* 2003, No. 38, pp. 139–73.
11 Catel, *Grenzsituationen des Lebens,* p. 112.
12 König, 'Das Problem der Euthanasie,' pp. 9f.
13 König, 'Das Problem der Euthanasie,' p. 10.
14 Karl König Archive.

Introduction: Karl König, Curative Teacher and Physician

1 König, 'Man and His Future,' *The Cresset,* Vol. 11, No. 1.
2 König, *Der Mongolismus.*
3 See p. 42.
4 See p. 44.
5 Scheler, *Schriften zur Soziologie und Weltanschauungslehre.*

3. The Purpose and Value of Curative-Educational Work

1 See Hanselmann, *Grundlinien zu einer Theorie der Sondererziehung.*
2 Homburger, *Psychopathologie des Kindesalters.*
3 Asperger, *Heilpädagogik.*

4. The Care and Education of Handicapped Children

1 R.A.H. Pearce, 'Crossed Laterality,' *Archives of Disease in Childhood*, Vol. 28, 1953, p. 247.
2 W. Haubold, 'Nachreifungsbehandlung beim Mongolismus', *Aerztliche Forschung*, Vol. 9, No. 1, 1955, p. 211.
3 A more detailed description can be found in König, *Der Mongolismus.*

5. Basic Issues of Curative-Educational Diagnostics and Therapy

1 Hanselmann, *Grundlinien zu einer Theorie der Sondererziehung*, p. 67.
2 Steiner, *Education for Special Needs*, lecture 6, p. 107.
3 Steiner, *Education for Special Needs*, lecture 6, p. 106.
4 Steiner, *Riddles of the Soul.*
5 Steiner, *Education for Special Needs*, lecture 6, p. 110.
6 Steiner, *Das Wesen des Musikalischem*, lecture 1.

9. Mignon: The History of Curative Education

1 Homburger, *Psychopathologie des Kindesalters*, p. 140.
2 Wassermann, *Casper Hauser,* conclusion of the dedication.
3 Löffler, F. 'Was zur Begründung des Institutes Lauenstein führte.'
4 Pickert, S. 'Von Rudolf Steiners Wirken bei der heilpädagogischen Arbeit,'
3 Steiner, *Education for Special Needs*, lecture 10, pp. 180f.
4 Steiner, *Education for Special Needs*, lecture 2, p. 47.

10. Adalbert Stifter and Curative Education

1 Steiner, *Education for Special Needs*, lecture 2, p. 39.
2 Steiner, *Education for Special Needs*, lecture 4, p. 87.

11. The Problem of Euthanasia

1 Quoted from Hase, *Evangelische Dokumente.*
2 Quoted from Hase, *Evangelische Dokumente.*
3 Catel, *Grenzsituationen des Lebens.*
4 Quoted from Hase, *Evangelische Dokumente.*
5 Quoted from Hase, *Evangelische Dokumente.*
6 Steiner, *Karmic Relationships,* Vol. VI, lecture of Jan 25, 1924, p. 18 (edited translation).
7 Steiner, *Fifth Gospel,* fifth lecture of Oct 6, 1913, pp. 94f (edited translation).

12. Euthanasia as a Challenge to Society Today

1 Ehrhard, *Euthanasie und Vernichtung lebensunwerten Lebens.*

Sources

Introduction: Karl König, Curative Teacher and Physician
First published in English translation in *The Cresset*, Vol. 12, No. 4, Michaelmas 1966.

1. Letter to the Parents of Camphill at Lake Constance
Letter on the occasion of the foundation of the Association of Parents, Relatives and Friends of Camphill in Germany. First published in Hans Müller-Wiedemann, *Karl König*, pp. 476–78.

2. To The Mother of a Down's Syndrome Child
Undated letter first published in König, *The Handicapped Child*, pp. 7–10.

3. The Purpose and Value of Curative-Educational Work
First published in *Camphill-Brief*, Christmas 1965.

4. The Care and Education of Handicapped Children
Based on a paper read at the Therapie Kongress in Karlsruhe, Germany, September 2, 1958. Translated by Peter Engel.

5. Basic Issues of Curative-Educational Diagnostics and Therapy
First published in *Die Drei*, Vol. 24, No. 3. Reprinted in Pietzner, *Aspekte der Heilpädagogik*.

6. The Three Foundations of Curative Education
Unpublished manuscript, written by Karl König for *Weleda Nachrichten*, No. 45, Christmas 1948. Publication could not be verified by the editor.

7. Modern Curative Education as a Social Issue
Transcript of Karl König's lecture at the Curiohaus Hamburg organized by the Christian Community (Nov 5, 1963). First published by Wolfgang Kohl in 1967. This reprint is based on that publication. Whether the transcript was proof-read and edited by Karl König is not known.

8. Curative Education as a Social Task
Lecture on November 13, 1963 in Cologne following an invitation by *Lebenshilfe für das geistig behinderte Kind* (Association of help for people with intellectual disabilities). Unpublished transcript edited by Karl König.

9. Mignon: The History of Curative Education
First published in *Der Beitrag der Geisteswissenschaft zur Erweiterung der Heilkunst. Ein anthroposophisch-medizinisches Jahrbuch,* Dornach 1950, pp. 219–43. Reprinted in *Aspekte der Heilpädagogik,* edited by Carlo Pietzner, Stuttgart 1959.

10. Adalbert Stifter and Curative Education
First published in *Das seelenpflege-bedürftige Kind,* 1955, Vol. 2, No. 1.

11. The Problem of Euthanasia
Transcript of a lecture at Föhrenbühl, November 1, 1965. Unrevised by Karl König. First published privately by Residential Special School Föhrenbühl (no date).

12. Euthanasia as a Challenge to Society Today
Transcript of a lecture at Föhrenbühl, November 14, 1965. Unrevised by Karl König. First published privately by Residential Special School Föhrenbühl (no date).

Bibliography

Arnold, Thomas, *Education of Deaf-Mutes*, London 1888.

Arnim, Georg von, *Bewegung, Sprache, Denkkraft* [Movement, speech, power of thinking] Dornach 2000.

Asperger, Hans, *Heilpädagogik*, Vienna 1952.

Breadley, J.W. *Doctor Barnardo*, London 1935.

Castiglioni, A. *A History of Medicine*, New York 1946.

Catel, Werner, *Grenzsituationen des Lebens: Beitrag zum Problem einer begrenzten Euthanasie* [Borderline situations in life; contribution to the issue of limited euthanasia] Nuremberg 1962.

Craig, W.S. *Child and Adolescent in Health and Disease*, Edinburgh 1946.

Dilger, F. *Giovanni Bosco*, Olten 1946.

Ehrhard, Helmut, *Euthanasie und Vernichtung lebensunwerten Lebens* [Euthanasia and the destuction of unworthy life] Stuttgart 1965.

Emminghaus, Professor H. *Die psychischen Störungen des Kindesalters* [Psychic problems in childhood] 1887.

Feuerbach, Anselm von, *Kaspar Hauser, Beispiel eines Verbrechens am Seelenleben des Menschen*. English: *Caspar Hauser, an Account* ... Allen & Tickner, Boston 1832.

Flugel, J.F. *A Hundred Years of Psychology*, London 1945.

Gordon, R.G. *A Survey of Child Psychiatry*, London 1939.

Guggenbühl, Hans Jakob, *Hilferuf aus den Alpen zur Bekämpfung des schröcklichen Kretinismus* [Appeal from the Alps for the fight against terrible cretinism] 1840.

Hanselmann, Heinrich, *Einführung in die Heilpädagogik* [Introduction to special education] Zurich 1932.

—, *Grundlinien zu einer Theorie der Sondererziehung (Helipädagogik)* [Outlines of a theory of special education] Zürich 1941.

Hase, Hans Christoph von, *Evangelische Dokumente zur Ermordung der 'unheilbar Kranken' unter der nationalsozialistischen Herrschaft in den Jahren 1939–1945* [Documents from the Protestant Church concerning the killing of the 'incurably sick' under the National Socialist government between 1939 and 1945] Innere Mission und Hilfswerk der Evangelischen Kirche in Deutschland, Stuttgart 1964.

Hein, Alois Raimund, *Adalbert Stifter: Leben und Werke* [Life and work] Vienna 1952.

Homburger, August, *Psychopathologie des Kindesalters* [Psychopathology of childhood] Berlin 1926.

Husemann, F. *Goethe und die Heilkunst* [Goethe and the art of healing] Dresden 1936.

Keller, A. *Kind und Umwelt, Anlage und Erziehung* [The child and the environment, disposition and education] Leipzig & Vienna 1930.

König, Karl *The Handicapped Child: Letters to Parents I,* London 1954.

—, 'Im Gedenken an Adalbert Stifter,' *Die Drei,* 1955 Vol. 25, No. 5.

—, 'Man and His Future,' in *The Cresset,* Vol. 11, No. 1.

—, *Der Mongolismus* [Down's syndrome] Hippokrates Verlag, Stuttgart 1959.

—, 'Das Problem der Euthanasie. Ein Wort zu Catels unseligem Buch,' in *Die Drei,* 1963, Vol. 33, No. 5.

Kretschmer, E. *Körperbau und Charakter* [Physique and character] Berlin 1929.

Krück-von Poturzyn, M.J. (Ed.), *Wir erlebten Rudolf Steiner. Erinnerungen seiner Schüler* [Experiences of Rudolf Steiner; recollections of his pupils] Stuttgart 1967.

Lazar, E. *Medizinische Grundlagen der Heilpädagogik* [Medical foundations of special education] Vienna 1925.

Löffler, F. 'Was zur Begründung des Institutes Lauenstein führte,' *Natura,* October/November 1926.

Müller-Wiedemann, Hans, *Karl König. A Central European Biography of the Twentieth Century,* Camphill Press 1996.

Pickert, S. 'Von Rudolf Steiners Wirken bei der heilpädagogischen Arbeit,' *Mitteilungen aus der anthroposophischen Arbeit in Deutschland,* Easter 1950.

Pietzner, Carlo (Ed.), *Aspekte der Heilpädagogik* [Aspects of curative education] Stuttgart 1959.

Rengger, H. *Dr med. L. Guggenbühl und seine Anschauungen über den Kretinismus,* dissertation, Zurich 1927.

Scheler, Max, *Schriften zur Soziologie und Weltanschauungslehre* [Writings on sociology and weltanschauung] Berne 1963.

Steiner, Rudolf, *Anthroposophy (Fragment),* (Complete Works (CW) 45), Steinerbooks, Mass. 2006.

—, *Education for Special Needs: The Curative Education Course,* (CW 317), Rudolf Steiner Press, London 1998.

—, *The Fifth Gospel,* (CW 148), Rudolf Steiner Press, London 1968.

—, *Geschichtliche Symptomatologie,* (CW 185), Rudolf Steiner Verlag, Dornach 1982.

—, *Karmic Relationships, Esoteric Studies,* Vol. VI, (CW 240) Rudolf Steiner Press, London 1971.

—, *Riddles of the Soul,* (CW 21), Steinerbooks, Mass. 2009.

—, *Von Seelenrätseln,* (CW 21), Rudolf Steiner Verlag, Dornach 1983.

—, *Das Wesen des Musikalischen,* (CW 283), Rudolf Steiner Verlag, Dornach 1969.

Strauss, A.A. & Lethinen, L.E. *Psychopathology and Education of the Brain-Injured Child,* New York 1948.

Strohschein, Albrecht, 'Die Entstehung der anthroposophischen Heilpädagogik' in Krück-von Poturzyn, *Wir erlebten Rudolf Steiner. Erinnerungen seiner Schüler,* pp. 216ff.

Tredgold, A.F. *Mental Deficiency,* London 1937.

Wegman, Ita, 'Über die Grundlagen in der Heilpädagogik,' *Natura,* October/November 1926.

—, 'Einiges über unsere heilpädagogischen Institute,' *Natura,* September/October 1928

Wurzbacher, Gerhard, *Leitbilder gegenwärtigen deutschen Familienlebens. Methoden, Ergebnisse und sozialpädagogische Folgerungen einer soziologischen Analyse von 164 Familienmonographien* [Sociological outline of current German family life] Dortmund 1951.

Zeller, W. *Konstitution und Entwicklung* [Constitution and development] Göttingen 1952.

Zilborg, G. *A History of Medical Psychology,* New York 1941.

Index

Karl König's collected works are being published in English by Floris Books, Edinburgh and in German by Verlag Freies Geistesleben, Stuttgart. They are issued by the Karl König Archive, Aberdeen in co-operation with the Ita Wegman Institute for Basic Research into Anthroposophy, Arlesheim. They seek to encompass the entire, wide-ranging literary estate of Karl König, including his books, essays, manuscripts, lectures, diaries, notebooks, his extensive correspondence and his artistic works. The publications will fall into twelve subjects.

The aim is to open up König's work in a systematic way and make it accessible. This work is supported by many people in different countries.

Overview of Karl König Archive subjects

Medicine and study of the human being
Curative education and social therapy
Psychology and education
Agriculture and science
Social questions
The Camphill movement
Christianity and the festivals
Anthroposophy
Spiritual development
History and biographies
Artistic and literary works
Karl König's biography

Karl König Archive
Camphill House
Milltimber
Aberdeen AB13 0AN
United Kingdom
www.karl-koenig-archive.net
kk.archive@camphill.net

Ita Wegman Institute for Basic
Research into Anthroposophy
Pfeffingerweg 1a
4144 Arlesheim
Switzerland
www.wegmaninstitut.ch
koenigarchiv@wegmaninstitut.ch